Higher Aspirations: So You Want An Advanced Degree?

Helpful Information for Students of Color

by

Frank Silvey Czarny, Ph.D. and C.J.H. Dorsey, Ed.D.

authorHOUSE

1663 LIBERTY DRIVE, SUITE 200
BLOOMINGTON, INDIANA 47403
(800) 839-8640
www.authorhouse.com

First published by AuthorHouse 08/06/04

ISBN: 1-4184-5097-9 (e)
ISBN: 1-4184-5096-0 (sc)

Library of Congress Control Number: 2004096351

Printed in the United States of America
Bloomington, Indiana

This book is printed on acid-free paper.

PREFACE

Who we are and what we know.

We are two people who have experienced the full range and wrath of institutional racism in the American education system. The intent of this book is not to drizzle hatred, hostility, or racial ill feelings. Rather, it is to share, as honestly as possible, some of the covert and overt forces that delay the academic progress of students of color in advanced educational degree programs. We share proven strategies personally used to facilitate a successful journey through a latently hostile educational system.

Okay, *so who are we?* Dr. Frank Silvey Czarny successfully earned a Ph.D. in Human and Organizational Systems in 2001. He is an African American who works as a human and organizational systems consultant. In 1973, Dr. Czarny received a Bachelor of Arts degree in Psychology, and later, in 1975 he completed a Master of Arts in Teaching. In addition, Dr. Czarny completed a second Masters of Arts in Organizational Development in 1998.

Dr. C.J.H. Dorsey completed her Ed.D. in Educational Leadership and Change. She is an African American who has 28 ½ years of state level program development, implementation and auditing experiences. In this capacity, she worked for the State of Washington, Office of Superintendent of Public Instruction, Olympia WA. Dr. Dorsey received a Bachelor of Arts degree in Education and a minor in Speech and Drama, 1964. Later, she earned a Masters in Education Administration, 1981.

Doctors Czarny and Dorsey have an enormous amount of professional career experiences. For instance, Dr. Czarny has worked as a caseworker for foster families and provided homes for developmentally disabled children. In this capacity, he provided psychological, emotional, and physical resources for several families. Similarly, Dr. Dorsey worked in community based organizations, establishing various social and educational training programs. In addition she provided services for families and individuals who were systemically classified as *disadvantaged*. Both Dr. Czarny and Dr. Dorsey have engaged in basic action research activities: *look, think, act*, as defined by Stringer (1996).

Dr. Czarny has also worked in the field of telecommunications. He was a telecommunications writer, instructor, and industry consultant. His vast educational background afforded opportunities to work on human relation, racial discrimination, and multi-cultural communication issues. Additionally, Dr. Czarny worked effectively with an array of executive, professional, and para-professional clients in these settings.

Analogously, Dr. Dorsey worked on equity issues in education. She wrote guidelines for working with special needs students. For teachers, counselors and administrators, Dr. Dorsey developed and implemented numerous statewide in-service educational training programs. She also conducted human relation workshops and conferences regarding civil rights and discrimination in education environments.

To the same extent, Doctors Czarny and Dorsey have taught in public school systems and have a grounded understanding of the educational process. In terms of instructional experiences, the teaching careers of Dr. Czarny and Dr. Dorsey nearly parallel at the college level. Dr. Czarny has developed and taught undergraduates and graduates courses, specializing in critical thinking, organizational behavior, and cultural diversity. Dr. Dorsey has assisted in the implementation of a community college adult basic education program, along with serving on numerous university special projects advisory committees. She has also served as a guest lecture for several graduate and undergraduate classes.

ACKNOWLEDGMENTS

I would like to acknowledge my mother, Doris M. Harris, for providing a proud lineage. She has served as a model for wisdom, strength, endurance, and courage on the battleground of racism in 20th and 21st Century America. I would also like to acknowledge my friend and benefactor, James Swanson, who constantly serves as an example of an excellent human being. His insurmountable belief in humanity and true joy in life has served as a constant reminder to have faith in human kind.

Dr. Frank S. Czarny, Ph.D.

DEDICATION

This book is dedicated to the memory of Dr. Marie Fielder, an outstanding Black educator, who insisted that the opportunity to obtain advanced educational degrees exist for all segments of the population, with out regard to race, color, national origin, gender, language or disabilities. She was an outstanding educational leader, a scholar, as well as an equity ambassador who walked her talk. She was a beautiful life role model, as well as a visionary educator. She was truly a nimbus of inspiration.

Dr. Fielder understood the educational struggles of students of color and relentlessly demonstrated the model for success. We shall always feel honored to have known Dr. Fielder, and will cherish her memory *forever.*

.

Table of Contents

List of Tables

List of Figures

INTRODUCTION

So you want an advanced degree…then remember this: ONLY THE STRONG SURVIVE AND ACHIEVE! The purpose of this book is to share some personal and professional insights on the subject of the acquisition of advanced educational degrees. This book also discusses challenges students of color confront, who are enrolled in predominately White colleges and universities, as they seek advanced educational degrees. It is important to note that the observations shared in this manuscript are a result of numerous years of experience.

For so many students of color, the decision to pursue an advanced degree is exciting. After all, having successfully completed high school, as well as an undergraduate degree, many students of color begin to entertain the idea of applying to graduate school for an advanced degree. In addition, career goals can reinforce academic goals in the process of acquiring an advanced degree. For example, today's competitive job market demands that candidates of color come fully equipped to vie for professional positions with solid experiences *and* supporting academic credentials.

Quite often, the student of color needs "inside information" in preparation for the overt and, especially the covert challenges and politics that await them. Perhaps, a student of color is the first in their immediate family to advance the educational ladder. The opportunity to excel is compelling. Another student of color, in contrast, may originate from a family that has a sustained history of high academic and career oriented success. Generally, the academic expectations from these families require the evolving adult to maintain family norms, traditions, and high educational achievements. Nevertheless, these young adults often encounter similar discouraging experiences when advanced degrees are sought. Either way hidden questions may linger.... Such as: What are the educational obstacles? How does one conquer these obstacles?

Once students of color have been accepted into a graduate school, the question of advanced degree acquisition is not immediately revealed to be problematic. The intellectual stage is set. The mission has been established; the commitment has been made. There may be a shared vision of success between students and their families. Graduation becomes a point of excitement: a psychological and emotional synergy begins to build. This book was written specifically to maintain that synergy and share some fundamental insights regarding the "pidgin pathway" students of color are often forced to encounter in order to achieve graduation.

Students of color must understand that faculty members are people like anybody else and are vulnerable to the same types of racial bigotry found outside of the educational setting. There is a *myth of the enlightened college professor*, and through a short learning curve, students of color must quickly understand and deconstruct the mythology. This myth provides an image of the enlightened college professor who is above the base tenants of racism.

Students of colors must study course guidelines carefully. If a certain assignment is found to be vague, clarification should be sought immediately. Clear understanding of course and faculty expectations is the key to academic success and performance must meet and/or exceed course requirements. A sound knowledge of academic products is developed by triangulation of student work: sharing them with a network of friends, family, and professionals before submitting them to the instructor. In addition, the student of color must be prepared to defend submitted assignments. When questionable remarks are returned on graded works, challenge the feedback in order to seek new understandings and clarifications.

Dr. Czarny ignored discouragement as a student. He understood that some instructors did not expect students of color to perform as well as other ethnic groups. To this end, he believes students of color must resist falling into the covert sabotage perpetrated by some instructors - the self-fulfilling prophecy. In addition, students of color must not fall into self-pity when a wrong has occurred against them. Dr. Czarny recommends to always have a 'Plan B' for overcoming institutional obstacles.

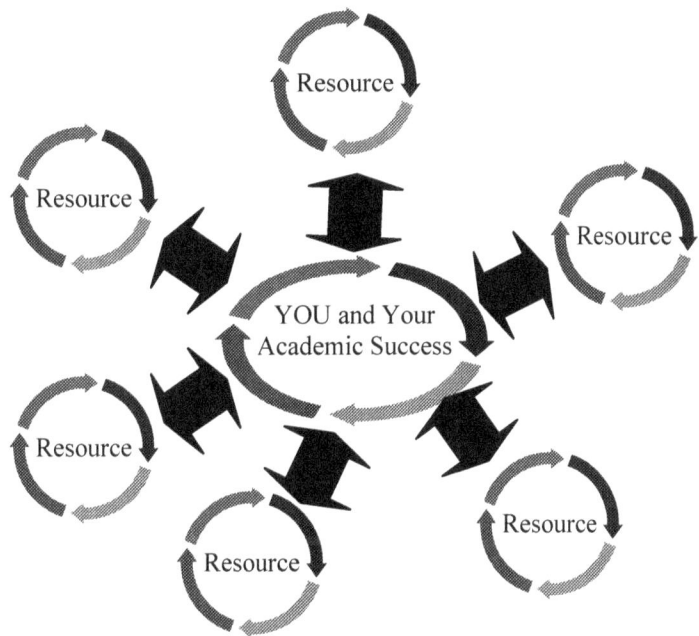

Figure 1. Orchestrated Leadership in Education.

These experiences have led him to develop an "organic" leadership model where individuals find success by effectively arranging wholesome resources around them. The process of creating supportive sub-systems for success is called "Orchestrated Leadership Theory (OLT)." This framework is used extensively in this book. See Figure 1.

For the purposes of this discussion, Orchestrated Leadership theory has been placed in the context of educational achievement and leadership. When viewed from this perspective, success in academic environment can be seen as a matter of surrounding yourself with a system of supportive resources. These resources enable you to achieve your unique educational milestones and objectives. Based on research concerning the forces that sustain African American families in hostile environments, Dr. Czarny discovered that individuals have the potential and ability to overcome severe environmental obstacles in the course of problem solving, decision making, and goal achievement (Czarny, 2001). Successful individuals effectively create a network of support systems and resources that serve as a safety net in times of conflict. As a private research and academic advisor, Dr. Czarny uses this approach to successfully coach individuals in the obtainment of their educational and personal goals, objectives, and visions.

Dr. Czarny believes students of color can achieve anything. He recommends to those who have achieved their academic goals to extend kindness and support to others. To those who assist and support, Dr. Czarny asks that they resist the urge to think they are superior to those who have the same color of skin who wish to take this educational journey. To those who aspire for an advanced degree, Dr. Czarny requests that once you get your degree, hopefully you realize that you are a better person, not a different person.

HISTORY

In order to understand the relationship between race and advanced degrees in America, understand the relationship between race and education in America. We use the case of the African American exclusively in this book, as the African American provides centuries of experience in America educational systems and sub-systems from which to draw. Looking at this issue from an African American point of view, it is imperative that a brief historical overview of the educational history of African Americans is presented. This historical information is significant in that it provides a broader awareness of why so few African Americans have acquired advanced educational degrees. Knowing the past in order to understand the present, to influence the future is critical.

Discrimination in education continued to be propelled toward African American descendants in America for generations (Bennett, 1984; Horton & Horton, 1995; Hughes, 1962; Jennings & Brewster, 1998). Numerous laws created continuity in school segregation as well as discrimination in southern and northern states (Dye, 1998). The system of segregation maintained and reinforced negative educational stereotypes regarding the intellectual abilities of African American students (Goldfield, 1990).

Racism created the harsh realities of discrimination in American culture, relative to the lives of African descendants beginning with their arrival in Jamestown, Virginia, 1619 (Bennett, 1984; Horton & Horton, 1995; Wilkinson, 1997). The institution of slavery in America was established utilizing Africans, after it was proven that they could survive the North American diet, temperature, and bacteria. Hence, the educational and social condition of African Americans today appears to be orbicular and thus traceable to the days of slavery and its hideous corollaries. It is hardly imaginable what deliberate efforts were made by Whites to dehumanize Black slaves in order to maintain lamentable life condition (Horton & Horton, 1995; Proctor, 1980).

Separate schools for Blacks were established in some communities; in others, such schools operated illegally. Some African Americans were *free* such as John Chavis in North Carolina, who actually taught school. In 1825, Chavis taught White students during the day and Blacks at night, for a small fee. Unfortunately, in 1829 North Carolina passed a state law that prohibited the availability of education for *all* African descendants. Therefore, pioneering Black educators such as Daniel Payne and John Chavis were forced to terminate their teaching activities (Wilkinson, 1997; Woodson, 1935).

Wilkson (1997) related the story of Prudence Crandall. Crandall was a Quaker schoolmistress during the 1830s who operated a girl's academy in Canterbury, Connecticut. She was moved to admit Sara Harris, the daughter of a Black family, to her school after reading Harris' story in The Liberator. Once Harris had been admitted to Crandall's school, a tremendous amount of harassment was initiated which ultimately forced Prudence to close her original school. Later, "in 1833 she reopened as a school for *colored* girls only, with young women from 20 well-to-do Eastern Black families" (pg.29).

Wilkinson (1997), records that Prudence Crandall faced renewed harassment in the form of white citizens' refusal to sell the Crandall School any supplies; denial of medical services to students; dumping of waste from a slaughter house on Crandall's home porch; shutting her and the students out of the church; stoning them; and seizing the girls on the street for outdated vagrancy laws and attempting to whip them. A local politician even came up with a provision of state law that prohibited "boarding or instructing any person of color not an inhabitant of the state without prior approval of the town." Crandall argued that this did not apply to incorporated colleges and academies and she was arrested for refusal to comply.

Crandall went on trial. She was convicted after Judge David Daggett instructed the jury that blacks were not citizens of the United States. (This statement later gave judicial precedent for the *Dred Scott* decision.) Eventually, Crandall's school was firebombed. Her case was set aside and she moved to Illinois. Prudence's conviction was never reversed but was erased from the record years later, and she was granted a small pension for the suffering endured.

Goldfield (1990) provided excellent accounts of "the way things were" regarding opportunities for African Americans. He stated that Black schools remained opened as much as seven months of the year and as little as three months in rural areas where local landowners determined the school-year calendar. White schools had sessions ranging from eight to nine months a year. Attendance at Black schools was poor because students often had to walk for several miles to get to their often one room school building. White children, on the other hand, generally had the convenience of school buses. Quite frequently, White parents paid for private bus services or boarded their children in town.

Black parents, according to Goldfield (1990), often had to supplement teachers' salaries and pay for materials that White children received through public funding. In addition, the hard-pressed sharecroppers or tenants held Black children out of school to work in agricultural fields or, because of shame due to inadequate clothing. Poor health, as well as the lack of truancy law enforcement, were two contributing factors for the limited participation of Black students in public schools.

Goldfield's research revealed that although some Blacks, especially in urban schools, learned something of their history in an 'off-the-cuff' manner, school officials designed curricula for Blacks that reinforced their place in southern society. Black children received training in "character building" or, in "courtesy, humility, self-control, satisfaction with the poorer things of life, and all the traits which mark a 'good nigger' in the eyes of the Southern Whites." The curricula, Goldfield (1990) discovered, generally avoided the subjects of civics and social studies. Although Vocational Education training comprised a major component of Black education, the curricula only provided training in menial occupations from domestic service to waiting tables. There was a concerted effort to discourage Blacks from learning or thinking about the "duties and privileges of citizenship" (Elkins, 1963). Consequently, Black children emerged from the public school system without the educational preparation that was necessary for career pathway and occupational success.

McLemore (1991) found that most Whites perceived Blacks as intellectually inferior and thereby used this perception to justify continued use of U.S. Supreme Court 1896 decision in the case of Plessy vs. Ferguson. The separate and uneven system of education seemingly produced Black students with limited abilities, and subsequently reinforced the negative opinions of Whites. Goldfield (1990) noted that in 1990, 98% of White southerners who responded to a Gallup poll were in favor of segregated educational systems. This widespread approbation provided very few reasons for political leaders to finance educational improvements for Black students. In fact, it appeared that most of the politicians were in agreement with Mississippi's Congressman James K. Vardaman, who declared that "money spent today for maintenance of public schools for Negroes is robbery of the White child of the advantages it would afford him, and you spend it upon the Negro what God Almighty never intended should be made" (Goldfield, 1990 p.75).

Southern education was another institutional support for White supremacy (Allport, 1980). Unlike the political or economic systems, the schools reinforced the generational continuity of race relations by initiating Black children into "their respective places" in southern society. It was not simply a matter of curriculum, the environment also left Black children with the indelible mark of inferiority. The physical surroundings, the long walks to school, the inadequate or absent educational materials, and the frequent interruptions in attendance were early lessons internalized by Black pupils (Wilkson, 1997).

Allport (1980), found that we often separate ourselves from people who *we* find uncongenial. Discrimination in education is like many forms of discrimination, usually a clandestine affair. However, he acknowledged that clandestine acts of discrimination were generally not true in southern states where most schools and colleges openly practiced 100 % discrimination.

The story of occupational discrimination in America was told in sweeping details by authors such as Davie (1949), Myrdal, (1944), and Saengar, (1953). They described how many firms would not hire the best person for the job if their skin color was dark, or if the person was Jewish, Catholic, or foreign born. Descriptions regarding the uneconomic aspects of discrimination was equally as revealing. For instance, it was not uncommon for Southern railroads to put an extra Pullman car on line, just to carry a single Negro passenger, so that White passengers would not have to spend a few hours of consciousness or unconsciousness in proximity to a Negro (Allport 1980).

The constitutional battle over civil rights and school segregation was most often remorseless. Dye (1998) cited The 14th Amendment, passed by Congress after the Civil War and ratified in 1868:

All persons born or naturalized in the United States, and subject to the
Jurisdiction thereof, are citizens of the United States wherein they reside. No
State shall make or enforce any law which shall abridge the privileges or
immunities of citizens of the United States; nor shall any State deprive any

person of life, liberty, or property, without due process of law; nor deny to

any person within its jurisdiction the equal protection of the laws.

Dye (1998) conveyed that the language of the 14th Amendment, established the legal foundation for Black people to receive the full measure of citizenship, as well as equality in America. During reconstruction and the military occupation of the southern states, some radical Republican Congressmen threatened to enforce all of the elements of the 14th Amendment. Furthermore, when Congress passed the Civil Rights Act of 1875, it attempted to legislate remedies in order to terminate racial discrimination in theaters, restaurants, hotels, and public transportation. Unfortunately, later in 1883, the U.S. Supreme Court declared the Congressional effort unconstitutional and thereby repealed the Civil Rights Act of 1875 (Horton & Horton, 1995; Kelly & Harbison, 1970).

During the 1800s, equal access to educational opportunities relevant to African Americans and other people of color was not an urgent nor confrontational issue. In fact, some would say that the lack of educational opportunity was the least of all problems facing the former slaves. According to Wilkinson (1997), the Freedmen's Bureau of Refuges and Abandoned lands was established and became operational on March 3, 1865. This bureau represented the first national welfare system. Thousands of Black people were homeless and unemployed in every state of the Union. Hence, many sought shelter and protection in towns and near military posts. Evidently, baseline survival was the focus, while educating Black children was a strong desire.

Once the Freedmen's Bureau of Refuges and Abandoned Lands became operational, it provided medical, employment, and educational assistance to poor Whites as well as the former slaves. However, according to Wilkinson (1997), the millions of dollars expended were not distributed on an equitable basis. One southern Bureau worker was quoted as saying, "We fed with government charity rations sixty-four Whites to one colored person" (p.45). The government gave White settlers millions of acres of land, while the Black refugees *hoped* to receive 40 acres per family (Horton & Horton, 1995; Wilkinson, 1997; Bennett, 1962).

In the midst of it all, educational opportunities for Black children slightly increased. As schools became available, Black parents strongly supported the education of their children in every way possible. Wilkinson (1997) and Bennett (1962) concurred that churches served as day and night schools for southern Blacks. Black people of all age groups (children, parents, and grandparents) attended schools as often as feasible.

According to McLemore (1991), in 1664, the state of Maryland adopted a law that condemned Black children to slavery for life. If they were born Black, or if their fathers were slaves, then the child was doomed to slavery for life. Legislation of this nature certainly assured a systematic feedback loop of racial discrimination and prejudice that was established years ago, and sustained for decades. The educational needs of Blacks were adequately met. In fact, Whites frequently burned down the few schools that were available to Blacks in the post-Civil War period (Comer, 1972; Goldfield, 1990).

Further indication of the lack of interest the White power structure had in Black education was given by school enrollment rates, median years of school completed, and the percentages of illiteracy in the population. In 1850, 1.8% of the Black children were enrolled in school as compared with 56.2% of the White student population. During the same timeframe, most Blacks in America were in slavery. The Research of Ducas and Vandoren (1970) revealed that some 20 years later, in 1870, 9.9% of the Black children were enrolled in school as compared with 54.4% of Whites. Even these enrollment estimates could be viewed as deceptive because Black students most often attended school for a maximum of 3 months per year versus 8 or 9 months per year for White students (Comer, 1972; Goldfield, 1990). Several generations later, Black student enrollment in 1950 was within 5 percentage points of White students. Given this historical perspective on racism in the educational setting in America, we now move to understanding the relationship between race and advanced degrees from an applied perspective.

UNDERSTANDING THE RELATIONSHIP BETWEEN RACE AND ADVANCED DEGREES

Introduction

Using Orchestrated Leadership, this chapter introduces you to six strategies for dealing with racism on the graduate level in higher education. To begin, you are shown how a system of racism is perpetuated in the educational setting. Then, you are provided two ways of checking for educational racism. On the *institutional level,* you are given a strategy for uncovering the racial "character" or "profile" of the graduate school. On the *programming level*, you are provided a method for checking the school's track record in preparing and supporting students of color for success. This strategy gives you a way for continually scrutinizing a graduate school's receptivity to students of color.

For the student of color, a system of educational racism can exert certain influential forces. These forces have the potential to play havoc over educational success for the student of color. The phenomenon of the self-fulfilling prophecy is an example of one such force of influence. In other words, low faculty expectations towards *you* may result in *your* representation as low performer. To this end, understand the invisible forces that may create

educational racism.

Figure 2. Orchestrated Leadership: Understanding Educational Racism

To counter the phenomenon, this section shows how to create a method of self-

analysis that increases probabilities for overcoming racism. An important part of the self-

analysis is your ability to create and sustain a dream. You are shown how to "lock-in" to

goals and avoid the imposition of lower expectations- by others and yourself. To conclude

the chapter, you are provided a strategy for developing your the powers of visualization through the use of prediction. Your ability to keep focused, stay on track, and maintain goals is essential to educational success. See Figure 2 for a graphic representation of the topics covered in this section. Remember that educational racism has the ability to detract you from reaching your dreams and with this in mind we now turn to a strategy for understanding racism on the educational setting.

Understanding educational racism

Understanding how past and common beliefs expressed in academia perpetuate racism.

One time I worked with a group of graduate students on an assignment. We had a suspicion that our psychology professor allowed his personal bias to affect the way he graded student papers in the class. We decided to conduct a very informal experiment. One student wrote a paper and as a group we prepared slightly different versions of the paper. We randomly handed out versions of the paper within the group. We put our names on the paper. The professor returned graded papers with consistently high marks- except mine- that had been given an average grade. I showed the paper to my parents and recounted the incident. My father looked at my mother and said, "it is history repeating itself." He walked out the room. Later, my mother explained to me that my father, her brothers, and uncles confronted many such experiences.

Be aware of the pervasiveness of educational racism through this incident. Understand the complexity of it. This kind of social and intellectual oppression ran through generations of my family history crossing dimensions of time and space. The grade given by the professor said that culturally – bounded *common beliefs* about African Americans can be unexpressed. However, common beliefs have the power to emerge in the evaluation behaviors of university faculty. Common cultural beliefs are deeply rooted in the American experience. Common cultural beliefs also exert a force of influence in dominant American society and also exert a force on smaller supporting sub – systems like the American education system. American society and it's sub-systems that perpetuate racism are fed by a deeper relationship between common beliefs and their historical underpinnings.

Common beliefs are fortified and compounded by yet another form of illogical thinking about African Americans: past beliefs. For example, negative stereotypes about Blacks are found in music, movies, news, as well as historical and contemporary literature. These venues consistently portray Blacks in terms of levity, servitude, violence, and crime. This imagery contributes to a social narrative of common beliefs surrounding the African American. In addition, stereotypic imagery reinforces *past beliefs* about Blacks (and Whites) in the American experience. One need only look at how Black imagery in movies continuously reinforces contemporary (common beliefs) and historical stereotypes (past beliefs). Essentially this is the code that sets the American stage about how Blacks are to be viewed and related - to in this country. Figure 3 shows how multiple venues in American experience play a regulatory role in perpetuating the myth of African American inferiority.

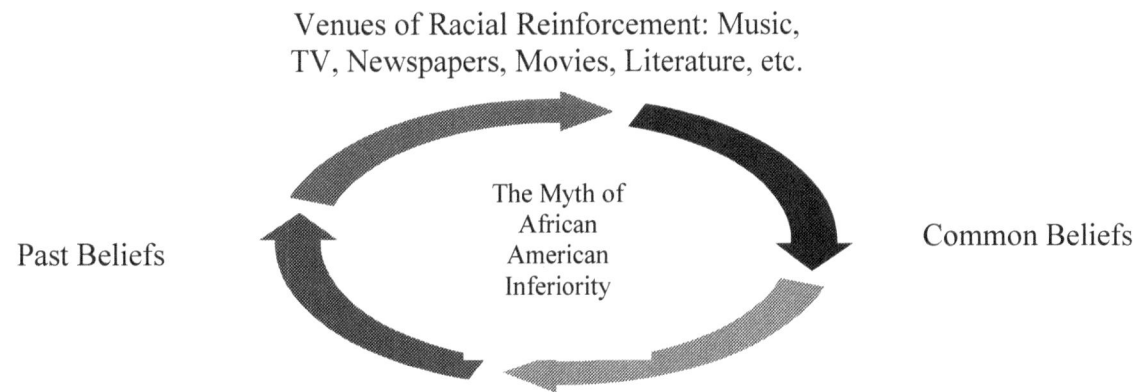

Figure 3. The Myth of African American Inferiority

Just as your body is a living system that needs food to sustain itself, a belief system based on the inferiority of Blacks continuously needs mental food in order to be replenished. For many people who are not African American, Black imagery found in movies, music, and newscasts is the only sustained contact made with Black folk. In large measure these negative representations feed common beliefs. Common beliefs continue to sustain past beliefs, and past beliefs remain unchallenged by the status quo. In the final analysis, a cyclical process has evolved that perpetuates the myth of Black stereotypes. The process has resulted in a system of self-fulfilling prophecy that has insured substandard delivery of services to African Americans across a range of American economic, political, governmental, and educational institutions. Now that we have established the systemic affects of institutional racism, the discussion moves to a consideration of the "racial profile" of an institution.

Learning the "racial profile" of the institution

Understand how to evaluate the educational receptivity for students of color on an institutional level.

It was five o'clock in the morning in my hotel room and a graduate student still wasn't done describing the horrors he'd experienced in his graduate program. We started talking right after dinner, about 7:00 P.M., and his litany of educational abuses never stopped. We were both students enrolled in the same graduate school. What held my interest and what was so disturbing about his accounts was that we had never met, yet I had experienced similar encounters and I was beginning to form a racial "profile" about the institution I was attending.

Here is one example of his experience:

> I applied to the graduate program and got accepted. I got the acceptance letter. Then they discovered I was Black during a conversation I had with an admittance counselor. Soon I received a call from the head of the program telling me they had changed their minds. I wasn't accepted anymore. I responded by saying that I thought it wasn't entirely legal. They reversed the decision and I was again admitted.

He went on to share another incident about an exchange between white male student and one white male faculty. They had jointly chuckled over offensive public remarks made to the student about "the purpose" of African women while conducting ethnographic research in third world settings. According to these white men, the purpose of African American women research subjects was that of a strictly sexual nature. There were students of African and African American descent in the room, who, after the discussion, took issue with the faculty member concerning the remarks.

The faculty member responded by becoming indignant. He said he was insulted and that he was tired of Black people always complaining about something. He turned to the young man who was presently recounting this event and said, "It is about time Blacks start taking responsibility for their actions." Blauner (1979), in this examination of institutional racism captures the dynamics of both critical incidents. He says,

> On one side we find the faculty defending its privileged position in the university, its distinctive academic values, and its generally liberal social philosophy. On the other side stand previously excluded student groups with an interest in establishing a base in higher educational institutions, and newly equipped with perspectives on race and society that in no small degree have grown out of the failure of civil rights liberalism to achieve its ends. p 258

The racial profile of the institution became perfectly clear at this time. I really didn't need any proof to validate if the accounts told by the student were true. I was experiencing exactly the same thing. I knew all too well that these acts were predicated on a "theory – in – use" that "white is right and if you're black, get back!" Theories – in – use are unseen understandings that are implicitly assumed to be culturally acceptable. Theories – in - use that perpetuate racism usually remain undetected until someone blows the whistle. "Espoused theories," in contrast, embrace those beliefs professed to be followed, but in reality, are practiced only as needed. Closely profile the racial climate of the institution. See Table 1.

Table 1

Profiling Institutional Racial Parity Theories

Concept	Recognize the gap between espoused theories (what is preached) and theories-in-use (what is practiced). Determine the degree of authenticity in terms of institutional claims of racial parity. It is essential to gauging personal success.
Some questions to ask:	1. Does the institution overtly espouse a racial parity theory? (preached) 2. Is espoused racial parity theory observable? (practiced)
Determine:	If there is a gap between what is practiced and what is preached, Beware! Prepare success strategies accordingly.
SOURCE: Adapted from – The fifth discipline (p. 202), by P. M. Senge, 1990, New York: Doubleday.	

Many schools- like many corporate organizations- espouse the theory of a diverse climate. In reality theories – in – use abound and can be observed on many dimensions. Lower admittance and graduation rates, racial flare-ups on campuses, and racial disparities observed in educational personnel are all barometers of local theories – in – use. These profiles speak to the true body of values and beliefs embraced by an institution. For these and many other reasons, minorities who consider going to white institutions are to keep their eyes wide open. Know that educational institutions have distinct racial personalities.

McClenney (1987) provides valuable insights for African Americans who wish to obtain formal education. See Table 2 for one piece of advice on decision-making.

Table 2

Using Strength in Numbers

Advice: Be aware of the personality of the institution		
If:	Then:	Or:
There is a personality clash with an institution you are currently in	A support group may help you survive and overcome	Move on to another institution with a more suitable personality
SOURCE: Adapted from – How to survive when you're the only black in the office (p. 39), by E.H. McClenney, 1987, First Associates Publishing: Richmond Virginia.		

McClenney says that it may be hard to believe, but less than 50 years ago, some states actually prohibited blacks from getting an education (pp.40-41). The root cause, according to McClenney, is that white controlled and run institutions really don't want to educate the person of color, in particular black men. However, a desire to preserve and fortify the black culture lay at the core of McClenney's arguments. In his discussion of black men, he asserts some institutions have personality traits that occasionally permit a few black men to complete a program. He also advances that many, (not all – my parenthesis), of these black men tend to be psychologically weak. He strongly feels these blacks have no courage or wisdom. White institutions systematically dissolve the strength and stamina of the black culture by reintroducing weak black graduates back into the black culture.

McClenney, in no uncertain terms, explains that other institutions have personality traits that are consciously determined to wipe you (the black person) out. He brings up the sad fact that these types of institutions have departments that are staffed with white people who believe in the inherent superiority of their whiteness and their intellect. Given McClenney's previous assertion about weak blacks, it is not hard to see that these departments may have blacks, and other minority groups that subscribe to the illusion of inherent superiority and intellect argument.

Bottom line, these departments are dangerous to you, your friends, and America, McClenney notes. "Academic Terrorism" is the term he uses to describe this phenomenon. Defined, it is vicious premeditated intellectual arrogance based on race (p. 42). See Table 3 for McClenney's advice on discerning the depth of an institution's racial personality:

Table 3

McClenney's Academic Terrorism: Exploring The Depth of an Institution's Personality

Ask the following questions:	
1	Is it a haven and home for the far left wing or far right wing thinking?
2	Is it an institution with no black faculty and administrators?
3	How many blacks are there in absolute and relative terms?
4	How many blacks are in your field of study in your department?
5	How many have graduated, and what are they doing now?
6	Is the faculty of the program made up of young white folks with only "academic" experience?
SOURCE: Adapted from – How to survive when you're the only black in the office (p. 42), by E.H. McClenney, 1987, First Associates Publishing: Richmond Virginia.	

McClenney states,

> "the black intellectual, the black who pursues a professional or academic degree beyond high school level, must be aware of the existence of academic terrorism. Think of the thousands of black athletes who have feathered the bank accounts of white universities but have not graduated." (p. 45)

It is important that students of color stand on firm ground when they enter a historically white institution of higher learning. Look to the strength, beauty and courage found in the ethnic American experience. Provide support to others who look like you. Be willing to listen to those are experiencing pain at the institution. Do not minimize or devalue their lived experiences. Offer advice and support only with permission and only to the extent that it does not put anyone in a questionable light. Understand the racial personality of the institution. Listen, observe, and understand the institutional difference between espousing diversity imperatives versus using diversity imperatives. Evaluate the possibility that you, as a student of color, may come into contact with someone who does not feel you are entitled to receive a graduate degree. So, create and use a support group, especially if you have discovered a racially hostile personality in the institution's graduate school program. We now move to a method of scrutinizing graduate programs.

Scrutinizing prospective graduate programs

Understanding how to evaluate the educational receptivity for students of color on a

programmatic level.

One time I was invited to create a program with a group of people in the same graduate school setting. I was the only student of color. Granted, it was a casual setting, yet the meeting was unruly, frivolous, loud, at points insulting towards participants, above all it was downright non-productive. I sat through the chaos experiencing a horror on two distinct levels. On a social level, I was horrified to see adults behave in such a childlike manner. On a professional level, I knew the people to be some of the most prominent, respected leaders in corporate North America. I surmised the educational climate at this particular institution fostered immaturity. Ironically, I was spared this exposure due to the aspect of "marginalization," the social out-grouping of certain segments of a population. This can happen in racially immature settings to students of color.

Below is a version of Smith's (1982) adult learning model modified for the graduate student of color. See Table 4.

Table 4

Graduate Schools and Five Characteristics For Students of Color to Consider

Characteristic	Description
1	Faculty members who are comfortable working with minority graduate students, have a sense of mission to make the program work for the student of color.
2	A comprehensive set of support services for the student of color that may include orientation activities, counseling, financial assistance, how-to-study help, and child-care facilities.
3	Flexible scheduling and curricular options oriented towards the minority experience.
4	An environment that supports multiple cultural perspectives and ways of knowing: there are locations for getting together on an informal basis, clear process for addressing conflict resolution and mediation for students of color.
5	Career assessment and job placement assistance that addresses the unique needs of students of color.
SOURCE: Adapted from – Learning how to learn: applied theory for adults (p. 121), by R. Smith, 1982, New York: Free Press.	

In a race-based society that practices degrees of rejection, to students of color, the sheer notion of being accepted *anywhere* is attempting enough to overlook the finer aspects of racial discrimination. *Resist the urge to jump at any institution.* Learn as much as you can beforehand about a school and choose your school wisely. Understand that there is a possibility that no one school could ever meet your total needs as a student of color. There are, however, certain characteristics the student of color should look for in advanced degree programs.

Continuously think in a critical manner with regard to your academic growth and development. Below is a theoretical model that describes a perspective on the relationship between students of color and educational institutions. Have a basic understanding of this relationship in order to detect deviations in administration and practice that impede or prevent the person of color from achieving her or his goals. See Table 5.

Table 5

Human Resource Frame for Graduate Schools that serve Students of Color

1.	Organizations exist to serve *human needs* of students of color (and students of color do not exist exclusively to serve institutional needs). Instead,
2.	Institutions and students of color, once admitted, need each other. Organizations need the ideas, energy, and talent that students of color provide, while students of color need the careers, salaries, and work opportunities that institutions provide.
3.	When the fit between the students of color and the institution is poor, one or both will suffer: The students of color will be exploited or will seek to exploit the institution or both.
4.	When the fit is good between the students of color and the institution, both benefit.
5.	Students of color are able to do meaningful and satisfying work while providing the resources the institution needs to accomplish its mission.
SOURCE: Adapted from – <u>Modern approaches to understanding and managing organizations</u> (p. 65), by L. G. Bollman & T. E. Deal, 1984, San Francisco: Jossey-Bass.	

Regardless of the school you select to attend, look for program components that bring out your best gifts, talents, and skills. Ultimately the responsibility of getting the most you can out of an educational experience depends upon you. Having a plan to move through the institution can not be over estimated. Knowing what to look for in a graduate program is important. Finding an institution that is the right "fit" for you requires careful scrutiny, so again- choose your graduate program wisely. In order to determine the right "fit," you must first understand yourself. The next discussion provides a method for conducting a self-analysis.

Designing your personal "character analysis"

Understanding how you can resist the force of self-fulfilling prophecy in academia.

Sometimes just one thing said or done makes things fall right into place. Such was the case with a multi – ethnic study group in which I participated. This group was in an advanced degree program. The first meeting, led by a person appointed by the institution, had no agenda or structure, it left the new students unclear and confused about program procedures. I reflected during this meeting and found it absolutely incomprehensible that as I entered the 21st century, I was in yet another system that had a "built-in" race based element that *delayed* my progress. It crystallized in this institutional appointee who lacked clarity, direction, and vision. Yet, through the grapevine, this person professed to be the self-appointed "savior" of black folk and the institution covertly subscribed to this way of thinking. Offline, about eight students decided to self – organize; have a second meeting in order to put together a plan of action for getting through the program. The group decided to meet at the house of one the team members.

The meeting occurred on a weekend, was a potluck, and the air was full of the aromas of good food yet the atmosphere was infused with a certain element of frustration. As the meeting progressed, expressions of despair and angst were released, plans were formed, tasks were assigned, and the study group adjourned. Including myself, three black faces remained in the room and were anchored to their chairs.

There was a thick silence in the room. I finally raised my head, a sigh came out of my mouth, like hot steam escaping a kettle whose lid has been left on far too long. Then, as if my thoughts had shot telepathically across the room, a sister raised her head, looked at me, and said," You know, you need to understand *in the final analysis* you are just a ("N" word) to white folks. You'll never quite get the best service. Once you understand that, you'll understand what's happening."

Later events proved these most powerful words to be true, and they served me well as I moved through the remainder of this particular educational system. These words were powerful because they put my educational experience into a cultural context. In the final analysis, *I began to see that my self-concept was totally different than the way others viewed me. In the final analysis, I came to learn how one social force contributed to this dissonance. It was a debilitating and silent force: the social narrative - at - large about Blacks in American society.* This social narrative was infused across social, governmental, corporate, and educational systems and it finally emerged in my learning team.

In the final analysis, this social narrative said to me that (non-African American) people in American systems could "get away" with providing American Blacks with marginal services and not be made accountable for such reprehensible acts. I considered this American social narrative an illogical mental set, based on a normative common fallacy. This fallacy is based on a presumed inferiority of Blacks and how they (do not) fit into the social fabric of power in mainstream America. Surmount this kind of ignorance by channeling your mental energies into crystallizing your future.

Sub - strategy: Crystallizing your future

Understanding how to "lock – in" on goals and avoid the academic imposition of

lower expectations.

Frame current educational aspirations within your cultural context as a person of color in America. In my case, it helped me to question if I really wanted to participate in a racially hostile graduate degree program. After considerable contemplation I decided to stay and tempered my actions in response to my new understandings. I needed to hold tight to my

dream. See Table 6.

Table 6

The Student of Color Deciding the Future

Step	As a Minority
1	What is your vision for the future?
2	What belief systems are pulling you back?
3	What needs to be done to move from where you are to where you want to go?
SOURCE: Adapted from – Discovering common ground (p. 294), by M. Weisbord, 1992, Berrett-Koehler.	

Exert some kind of control over hostile conditions that manifest in lack of

programmatic direction. Take an *honest* look at current reality. Be willing to look at any

covert subconscious forces as well as overt social forces that converge to delay the

attainment of educational and professional goals. Assess what you have to work with, and

through that assessment determine what actions need to be taken for goal achievement.

The work of Senge (1990) describes a process of self-analysis within a larger process

called personal mastery. It works on the concept of "tension." Self-analysis starts with where

you are now and examines environmental forces that play a part in delaying or facilitating

the realization your personal dreams. In the process of self - analysis debilitating and

facilitating belief systems are examined. Beliefs are portrayed as clouds in Figure 4, these

represent forces that either pull a person back or pull a person towards their desired goals.

Figure 4 also represents a model that enables the process of dignified self – directed

growth and goal acquisition to be viewed, analyzed, and recreated. Self – determination is

vital to the success of the student of color and this success is based on the power to envision the future. Recognize that there are internal and external environmental forces that have to potential to delay your progress. Ethically manipulate these forces to serve your interests.

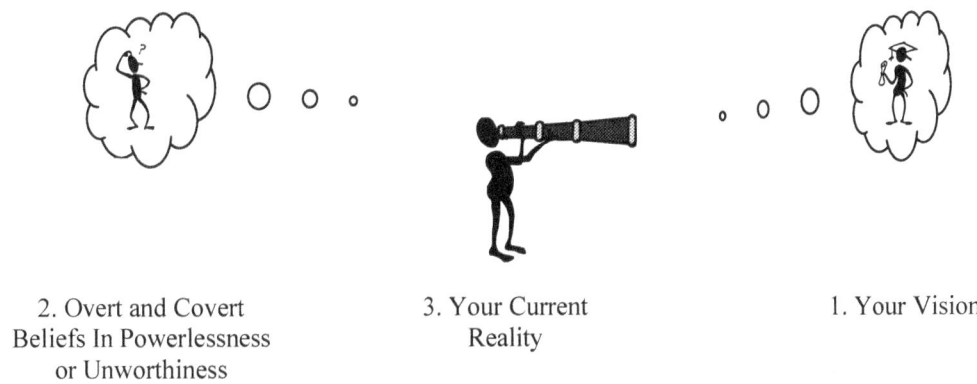

2. Overt and Covert   3. Your Current   1. Your Vision
Beliefs In Powerlessness   Reality
or Unworthiness

Figure 4. Current Reality and Students of Color

At the same time, identify and build on the positive forces that enable you to move forward. If problems are encountered in your educational journey, first and foremost, focus on the final destination. Keep your eyes on the prize be persistant and resilient in goal achievement. As a student of color you will be discouraged in 101 different ways from 101 different sources, both informal and formal.

This discouragement can take the form of someone else deciding your future for you. For example, in the movie "X," a scene shows Malcolm X with his grade school teacher. We see the process of self-fulfilling prophecy at work in this scene. This phenomenon takes the form of low teacher expectations. The teacher encourages Malcolm to be a janitor, and dissuades him from realizing his dream to be a professional. In my own case, a counselor told me I would never make it in college. Instead of buying – in to the deception, I just let the negative words just roll off my back, dismissed the negative expectation. I took action to realize my vision to be a professional and this meant keeping my eyes on the prize. I spread my wings and I flew. If negative thinking is experienced in academic progress, put it in context with professional vision, and affect positive action that moves toward goal acquisition.

Use critical thinking as a tool for visualizing academic and professional terms. Write down all the pressures that provide a distraction from vision. Then note all the actions needed to reach the vision. Is there a need to create an action plan for dealing with forces that compel you to lower your vision? Can the vision be reached by strengthening certain life-space forces? What resources are available and/or needed to reach the vision? After earnest contemplation, is there a need to re-design the plan reaching the vision? These are all important questions to ask yourself when crystallizing your future.

The process of keeping focused also involves the ability to make predictions about your present situation and future states of being. Consider the following account that shows how the power of prediction can help put things in their proper perspective during times of conflict, denial, and confusion.

Sub - strategy: Predicting in order to progress

Understanding how to recognize and manage real-time forces of deception and

refocus on original goals.

One time I had a study group member come over to my house and work on a joint project. During a coffee break in my kitchen we discussed how it was nearly impossible to second guess how a faculty or staff member would react to any request submitted by a student of color. We continued to talk and with regard to completing academic requirements, we discovered a joint experience of entrapment. This entrapment consisted of broken promises, misinformation, incomplete information or no information, and misdirection. We agreed that when the student of color acted on this faulty information, the consulting faculty or staff member would send an humiliating message, copied to academic advisors that suggested student dishonesty in, for example, by – passing a step in the program. We surmised the information would be entered into the student's "file" as future ammunition for heaven knows what.

We both agreed that although we could not guess real – time faculty and staff reactions to requests, we *could* predict the consequences of deception. A deck of tarot cards appeared on the table and a "reading" was obtained on individuals that had tried to humiliate us. There was one administrator who had been especially negative to both of us. When the name of this administrator came up in our discussion, the "Tower" card was pulled from the deck. A figure was shown falling from a burning tower. Two months later, the person in question left the institution under questionable circumstances. The point of this story is not to encourage the use of tarot cards in your educational journey. Instead the point is to use the power of prediction as a means for creating context, and for re - focusing on original vision.

In essence the breakfast table discussion was an object lesson on strategic planning on racially hostile academic environments. The discussion surveyed the kind of environment we were in, and brainstormed different ways of conflict resolution. Using systems thinking principles, we formulated a "predictive retention hypotheses" identifying social, cultural, organizational, and economic forces that could exert the force of an institutional delay up to and including dismissal of the graduate student of color. See Table 7.

Table 7

Predicting Changes in the Environment of the Student of Color

Step	Activity
1	FORM a limited number of goals not to exceed five-six years for predicted educational changes.
2	IDENTIFY discriminatory boundaries beyond local control in these goals.
3	IDENTIFY affirmative forces that diverge and overlap in the goals.
4	CLARIFY complexity and contradictions introduced by racial narratives (i.e. unseen or hidden agendas fed by contending cultural stereotypes)
5	IDENTIFY problems fed by cultural conflicts of interest: devise alternative ways about how to redefine them.
6	REDEFINE problems in rational operational terms in ways that will allow the creation of alternative plans of action.
7	LINK predictions to plans of action and present conditions.
SOURCE: Adapted from – <u>Discovering common ground</u> (p. 89), by M. Weisbord, 1992, Berrett-Koehler.	

Based on this information the breakfast table discussion resulted in a multiplicity of ways for looking at one's situation and planned ways of using policies and procedures to one's best advantage. In this case, making sure staff and faculty complied to organizational and regulations- when it came to fair treatment and evaluation of educational products- turned out to be a blueprint for success.

Life is a continuous process of change. Progressing in life involves using the ability to envision the future and this must involve the power of prediction. Envisioning the future through prediction is part of critical thinking and it enables effective navigation of change. Stay on top of intellectual transformation by developing skills of prediction. Prediction helps adaptation to change with a basic framework for dealing with the unknown. Figure 5 outlines a process for prediction in an environment of change. Create a force field analysis diagram for each step of this method. The purpose of the diagram is to pinpoint elements that may resist and assist the individual in goal acquisition. The diagram can be used in the academic arena in developing personal strategies for identifying and dealing with inhibiting forces and making optimum use of promoting forces.

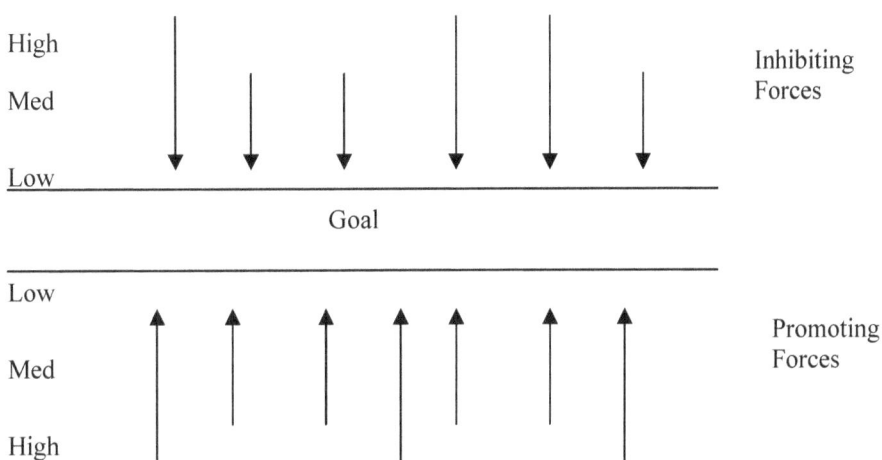

Figure 5: Force Field Analysis for Goal Acquisition

Instructions

Force Field Analysis for Goal Acquisition

Step	Action
1	IDENTIFY the goal to be analyzed.
2	BRAINSTORM and list all the possible promoting and inhibiting forces which would generally relate to area unique to your situation, for example: • Forces of Racism • Internal personal forces • External socio-economic forces • Familial forces • Spiritual forces
3.	EVALUATE the strength of each of these forces
4.	MATCH promoting forces which balance or overcome inhibiting forces.
5.	TRANSFER all the forces to the diagram by matching subject to degree of force.
6.	DEVELOP action plan

This tool of analysis can be used on two levels: private and public. By examining the public (espoused theory) and the private (theory-in-use), this kind of analysis unfreezes correspondingly private and public agendas that oppress personal progress. On a private level, this analysis unfreezes those unconscious or subconscious mental sets that work against personal growth. On a public level, it is a process that allows you to unfreeze the ice of indifference, intolerance, ignorance, or uncertainty. Visualize private and public agendas as forces to be handled. Channel, reshape, or circumvent these forces in order to create a desirable experience that works. In my own situation, once I was able to identify those forces (people, places, and things) of low institutional expectation, I was able to gather, reshape, and capitalize on forces (people, places, and things) that facilitated personal success. Once I reformed these forces into a positive experience, I re-froze them and integrated them into my life. This concept is captured by the work of Kurt Lewin, a social scientist who studied casual forces. The phenomenon of unfreezing, moving, and freezing into new operational levels is shown in Figure 6.

Figure 6: Lewin's Law

You have choices in your educational development. If you are a minority, and you are experiencing disharmony in your educational experience, conduct a self-analysis to capture debilitating social and personal forces – in – use. Put a plan together to deal with them. Let the final analysis be *your* final analysis, and let your final analysis be the beacon

that guides you to your educational goals.

Chapter Summary

When entering the arena of advanced degrees, the student of color must assume an holistic approach to obtaining success. This means undertaking a thorough process of research, analysis, and diagnosis of prospective educational programs. Frame this in a perspective of the Orchestrated Leadership model. Identify the numerous resources in your environment that will increase the probabilities of academic success. I have never encountered the "perfect" white educational institution. With this in mind, the student of color must evaluate the racial climate of candidate institutions. On a deep, psychological level, evaluation is important because it infers that critical thinking is used in determining your educational and occupational development and future. If your particular set of circumstances move you to a narrow range of prospects and/or an institution that has a history of racial bigotry, then the tools and strategies identified by using the Orchestrated Leadership model will give you ideas on how to move forward in these situations.

The next section of this book is based on the assumption that racism is an act of war waged by humanity upon itself. The upcoming section talks about winning this war. Given this perspective, you are presented with powerful strategies used for navigating racial hatred. The first strategy deals with effectively understanding your reality and how your internal experience can be used as a barometer for navigating change.

ENGAGING INSTITUTIONAL MENTAL WARFARE AND WINNING!

Introduction

There is a subtle race war occurring in American institutions of higher learning. It is important that the student of color be equipped with the proper accouterments to do battle. This chapter discusses the engagement in institutional warfare and how to win. The internal experience of the student of color must be absolutely sound and this chapter starts with a strategy for linking psychological and emotional states to educational progress. This chapter is based on the assumption that when the student of color possesses sound internal experience, the student can readily identify short and long term solutions in response to diversionary tactics. In the context of this book, diversionary tactics are those acts originating from agents in an institutional setting that delay the progress of students of color. Diversionary tactics essentially portrait the unwitting student of color as inadequate, in reality a scapegoat for educational irresponsibility, while the perpetrator fanes innocence.

Another essential survival skill is the ability to keep eyes wide open at all times. A strategy is provided that assists students of color in analyzing what is known in complex educational settings. In my experience, academia is known for cloaking its racism in complex-sounding terminology meant to simultaneously impress and confound the listener. A strategy is presented which helps the student of color deal with innuendo and read between the lines. It is essential for the student of color to accurately interpret and clarify remarks that carry the power to potentially debilitate intellectual, psychological, and emotional development. In the realm of social interaction, the student of color must develop the capacity for x-ray vision. A strategy is presented that enables the student of color to understand unseen relationships in educational settings.

This book is also based on the assumption that sound, realistic personal planning is essential to educational and ultimately occupational success. The concept of the "educational self," inspired by the concept of "occupational self" (Greenhaus as cited in Stevens-Long & Commons, 1992, p.202-3), is introduced and examined. This chapter also discusses a strategy for developing and engaging the educational self through the planning of personal milestones. A strategy is also provided for working with educational integrity.

Figure 7. Orchestrated Leadership: Engaging in Institutional Warfare and Winning

Integrity ultimately reflects in the quality of your knowledge base as a professional in the working world. To this end, a strategy is provided which enables the student of color to ground learning on an identified set of personal values. These values are to be routinely revisited during the educational phase of occupational development. This chapter concludes with a strategy for dealing with the social realities of being a student of color in America. A model of Orchestrated Leadership, Figure 7, gives a graphic representation of the strategies discussed in this chapter. We now move to dealing with the psychological and emotional experiences of denial and confusion for the student of color.

Dealing with denial and confusion

Linking your psychological and emotional states to educational progress.

A client encountered a lack of mentorship in a specific graduate program and was describing the frustration: The client made the following remark:

> "Well, I *really* don't want to burn any bridges, you know. I mean, I have to be political. You know, he is my academic mentor and although he hasn't given me any direction since I started the program two years ago, I don't want to get him mad at me by letting him go."
>
> -Delayed Graduate Student of Color

This remark was made to me by one of my clients, an African American graduate student. It was made during an initial problem – framing exercise in the opening sessions of a consulting relationship. In this student's particular graduate program each student was assigned a mentor. With respect to the specific graduate school program, the mentor was supposed to support the student in good and bad times. It just wasn't happening for my client.

I noticed one inductive form of reasoning in my client's account. Among many dynamics I discerned a far – fetched hypothesis that being political was linked in instrumental ways to educational achievement. To the client, being political meant not raising the ire of educational representatives, even if representatives were remiss in the performance of their professional responsibilities. The client, coincidentally, had observed little progress with other minorities who had had this mentor. The client also received information and warnings concerning this mentor from various related and unrelated sources. In this environment these resources told a story of mentor neglect and arrogance, perpetrated consistently towards students of color.

From my perspective, I was forming another mental picture about the "racial personality" of an institution. I had hypothesized that at some deep, covert level a psychological contract had been made between the faculty mentor and the institution. This contract manifested in the behavior patterns of this faculty member. Unwitting students of color were submerged into a process of delay and confusion that would ultimately impact institutional drop – out and retention rates *for* students of color. My client had created a political hypothesis to excuse the practice of prejudice. Could a plausible hypothesis be that the mentor was a flat – out bigot? I advance that a plausible hypothesis is sometimes the hypothesis that the student of color simply does not want to believe.

Looking back, my client was thrilled to enter the graduate program. As time passed, joy turned into denial. Other students who had started with my client progressed in the graduate program. Yet, my client clung to one of the organizing principles of self – directed learning upon which the program was based. The principle was that each student

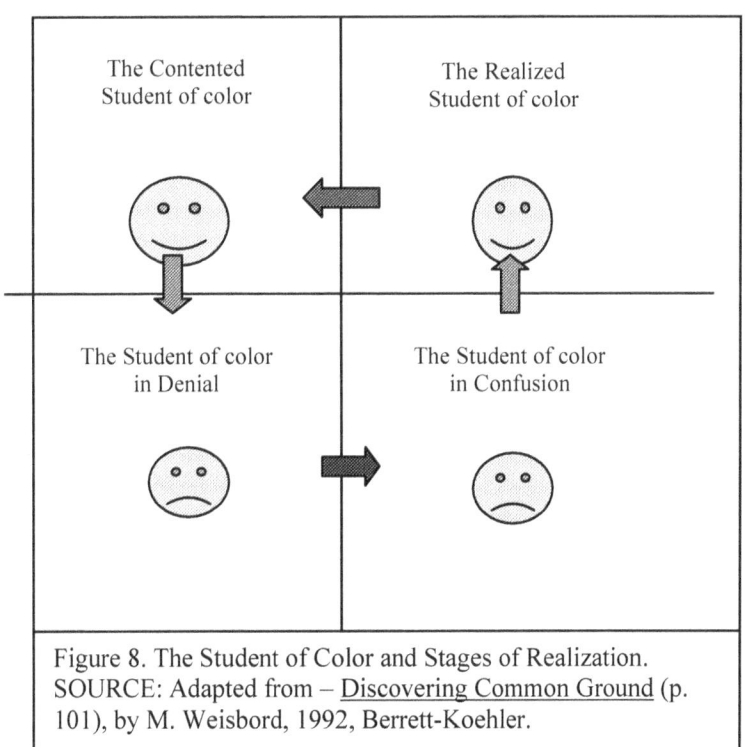

Figure 8. The Student of Color and Stages of Realization.
SOURCE: Adapted from – <u>Discovering Common Ground</u> (p. 101), by M. Weisbord, 1992, Berrett-Koehler.

Table 8

<u>Explanation for Stages of Realization</u>

Stage	Description
Contentment	This is when the student of color likes current conditions. When agreeable conditions change, the student of color moves into a state of denial.
Denial	The student of color in this stage will not accept a current academic reality that is not in their favor. They stay in this stage until they have the strength and courage to look at their fears and anxieties. Once this is done, they move to confusion.
Confusion	The confused student of color is busy sorting out how to recover a state of equilibrium in the academic setting. The advent of anxiety, or "Gestalt" (revelation) signifies a readiness to learn.
Realization	The passage to Realization leads from Denial through Confusion.

progress at his or her own rate. For my client the principle turned into a myth that eventually became an anchor of delay. It hung around the client's neck like an albatross. This condition expressed itself in a state of denial that allowed status quo conditions of faculty-induced delay to continue. Eventually, my client began to observe and compare notes between those who were experiencing progress and those experiencing delays.

The client then became confused and realized that something had to be done. As a student, my client started looking for ways of moving forward, alternatives for getting through the system. My client contacted me and we are now experiencing dramatic degrees of success. These victories reinforce the will to continue. However, the process of staying aware, keeping on top of things, and avoiding the "pull" to slip back into states of denial and confusion has been a continuous challenge in a covertly racist environment. The Figure 8 shows how it works.

Are you going through a hostile educational experience and wondering if you're seeing things accurately? For the student of color, pursuing educational development perhaps implies experiences of joy, disappointment, chaos, and transformation on many levels. View the experience of change as a stage – based phenomenon to be understood in psycho - emotional states. It is a cyclical process. In the human experience, the "Stages of Realization" approach is one form of self-evaluation. Staying in touch with "Self" helps to effectively evaluate situations, problem-solve, and make effective decisions to break cycles that delay. The discussion now moves to a closer examination of diversionary delay tactics and educational responsibility.

Shifting the burden where it belongs

Identifying short and long term solutions to diversionary delay tactics.

"I don't really think you are a fit for this program," the voice on the other end of the phone line said. It was about nine o'clock in the morning and I had already been studying for three hours straight. I had just entered a graduate program and upon hearing the remark, all I could think was "here we go again." The person calling was the head of the graduate program, and I guess the comment was the straw that broke the camel's back. I replied, "There's not a damn thing wrong with me. If there's anything wrong, it's the structure of this program."

Structure is the operative word. Many individuals and institutions in America select to blame the African American for real (and conjured) troubles observed in the African American experience and the large dominant American culture. Instead of tracing the root causes of these troubles to discriminatory practices infused in institutional structures, policies, and "groupthink" that deny equal opportunity, it is much easier for the attacker to blame the victim and shift the burden (Senge, 1990). The so – called troubles of the African American experience can be viewed from a perspective of complexity, that is, from a perspective of being able to see the various dimensions of discrimination from various perspectives in the structures of systems that oppress. When a student of color experiences oppression, the student must identify and understand the multiple forces that feed the oppression. It is a process of root cause analysis and it gives the student real data to get a *clear picture* of what is going on and construct a plan of corrective action.

Generative Aspects

When I told the department head that "if there's anything wrong, it's the system," I was referring to the generative aspects of the educational system in which I was enrolled. Mentally, I questioned what would compel a leader in an educational system to discourage a newly admitted student of color from obtaining an advanced degree. I asked myself, "What sub - system of core values and beliefs would generate and endorse the behavior?" I selected to seek to understand acts of discrimination by looking at institutional and personal norms, values, and beliefs that emerge in human interaction. Taking this approach stops the process of taking responsibility for the hatred of others. Gauge your responses accordingly.

Responsive Aspects

When I said to myself "here we go again," I was referring to the responsive aspects of the educational system in which I was enrolled. On an historical level, different educational programs had responded to me with a similar pattern of discouragement. On a contemporary level I was beginning to notice that the large majority of faculty members tended to keep their "distance." When your educational process is delayed, look for the pattern of oppression in the situation. Look at phenomenon in terms of "origin" and "direction" in your experience. Begin to explore trends among people who look like you, discover that the problem does not lay with you. Collect and save this information as psychological data to buttress self-esteem and confidence. Coupled with sound educational products, wisdom is gained and probabilities of success increase because your case is based on observed reality, collect data, and facts.

Event Aspects

I viewed the statement of the department head as a reactive stance against my progress as a graduate student. Since I had not been able to even demonstrate my abilities before the statement I was led to believe that the statement was an expression of prejudice based on some set of unknown, stereotypic data. When trying to problem-solve and make decisions, again, understand the originating and terminating points of oppression in an event. Avoid operating at a "who did what to who" event level. Instead, acknowledge these forces and problem solve from a structural perspective using the model found in Figure 9.

Structural Problem - Solving

When determining the causes of educational delay, start from the event, and look to see if the similar behavioral patterns of delay are demonstrated in other ways on a larger context. Look to see what aspects or conditions within the educational system contribute to the behaviors that delay your progress. Approach problem – solving in a manner that allows you to gain some distance from the event and view it from multiple perspectives. In this way, you can explore the causes that contribute to your delay and design alternative solutions to move through the system.

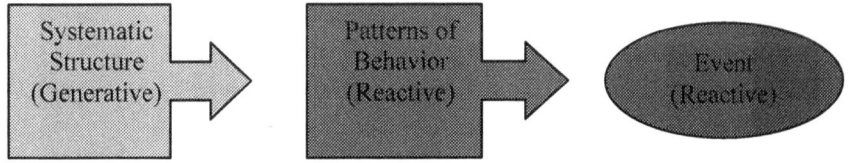

Figure 9. Senge's Multiple Levels of Explanation In A Complex Situation.

Table 9

Focus on Levels of Explanation

Explanation Level	Focus is on:
Event	"who did what to whom"- doom their holders to a reactive stance"
Patterns of behavior	seeing longer-term trends and assessing their explanations
Structural	answering the question: "What causes the patterns of behavior"

SOURCE: Adapted from – The fifth discipline (p. 52), by P. M. Senge, 1990, New York: Doubleday.

Consider this exploration a root cause analysis that examines educational structure. This means looking at the institutional expression of equality though standard operating procedures, as well as staff, faculty, and student attitudes, beliefs, and values. Understand how this mental activity can drive patterns of behavior across institutional time and space. Equip yourself with explanations for why certain events occur around you and to you. Enable yourself to logically evaluate a situation after making an assessment by answering what causes certain patterned behavior witnessed within an academic setting.

In the original phone call of the department head, the symptomatic problem was: "How could this person possibly know that I was not a "fit" before I was even able to demonstrate my abilities? I label it as a "symptomatic problem," because I featured there were deeper, casual forces at play and I was only witnessing the tip of the iceberg. I advanced it was a form of illogical thinking, a hasty generalization, where the department head simply did not have enough academic evidence upon which to base the generalization. Upon hearing this information, I decided to develop an array of "symptomatic solutions." For example, I could have "owned" the erroneous information and withdrawn from the program, or I could have put the onus back of the shoulders of the owner and give *myself* permission to complete program requirements, or I could have done nothing. I selected to give myself permission to complete program requirements.

One of the side effects of all this mental maneuvering was that it took time to figure out what to do. It was time that could have been allocated to the completion of my studies. Therefore the act of the department head introduced a delay in my educational progress. My fundamental solution to this situation was to carefully follow program directions and requirements. In my case, this proved to be the most efficient means of getting through the system.

Sub Strategy: Designing your learning system

The work of Capra (1996) illustrates this process from a systemic perspective. There are many types of systems in this world. For example, there is the respiratory system, the solar system, governmental systems, beliefs systems. Viewed on another level, *people* have a system or way of going about their business in the world. For the graduate learner this means, for example, a system or method of tackling assignments, reading materials, writing essays, thinking critically, and completing program assignments… even if the method as having no method at all- its a pattern of doing things. It's different for each person. Here is a symbolic example of a learner's system:

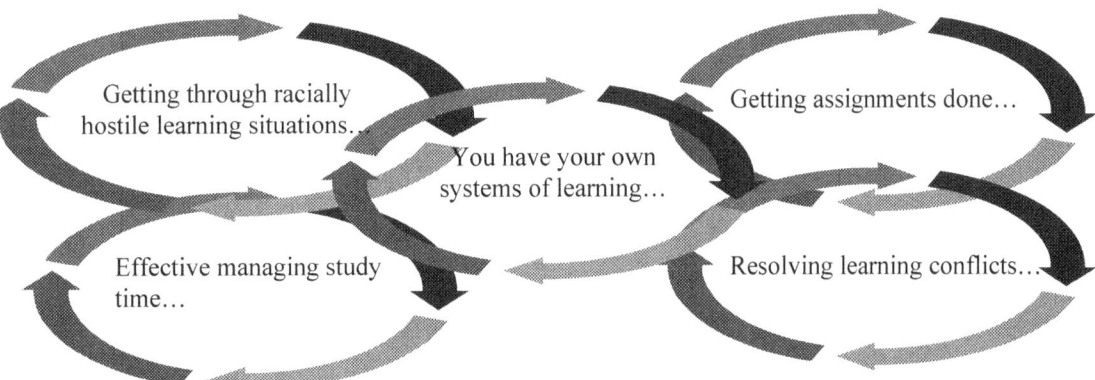

Figure 10. Sub-systems within a System of Learning

The ovals represent dynamic intersecting behavioral sub-systems, forces that intermingle, converge, and constitute your overall personal system of learning. In turn each one of these sub-systems has dynamic elements that push, pull, twist and turn to keep your personal learning system on target. Let's take a deeper look inside one sub-system.

Sub-strategy: Knowing positive and negative behaviors

Suppose we were taking a look at the sub-system of behaviors a person uses to navigate a racially hostile educational environment. What would be some of the elements instrumental to getting through a hostile educational environment? Review Figure 11.

System: Getting through a hostile educational environment:

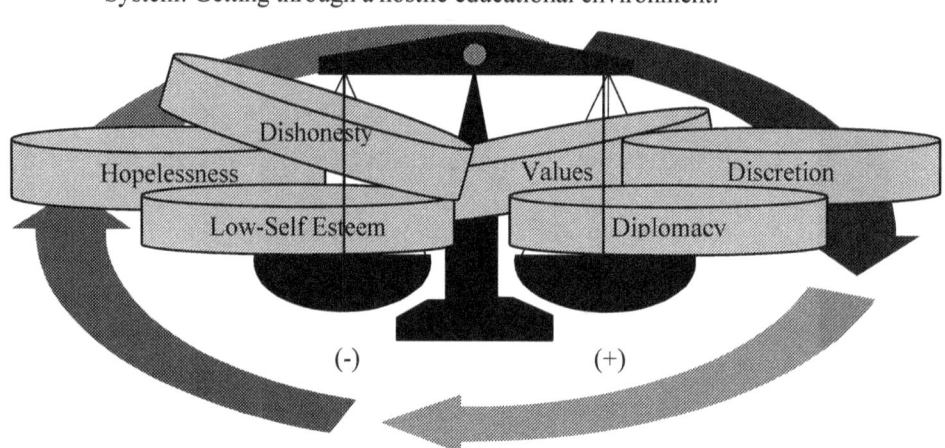

Figure 11. Some Elements That Affect Getting Through Hostile
Educational Environments

In Figure 11, labeled coins represent a sample of elements that constitute the sub-system of behaviors a person may use to navigate a racially hostile educational environment. To add a sense of dynamics, coins rest on a balancing scale which has negative (-) and positive (+) valances: coins on the negative side pull a person away from the goal while coins (elements) on the positive side pull a person towards the goal. The arrows represent a causal feedback loop (Capra, 1996) where co-mingling of positive and negative elements regulate the degree to which you navigate a hostile educational situation… and stay on course to reaching your goals (Senge, 1990). The rate of advancement through external environments is dependent upon the degree to which casual forces- internal and external- activates the dynamic balancing of these elements. For example, discrimination can be seen as a negative casual external force while your degree of self – esteem can be seen as a positive casual internal force. Both forces influence your navigational methods.

Sub-strategy: Recognizing environmental manifestations

To possibly circumvent racism in academia, and to gain a holistic picture of academic racism, it is important to capture outward manifestations of this kind of human activity. These manifestations can be understood in terms of: "knee jerk response" to addressing racism (i.e. identification of racial discrimination); symptomatic solutions ("quick fixes"); understanding the side effects of academic racism; associated delays; and development of fundamental solutions. This can be summarized in the form of a box as shown in Figure 12.

- Symptomatic Problems
- Symptomatic Solutions
- Side Effects
- Delays
- Fundamental Solutions

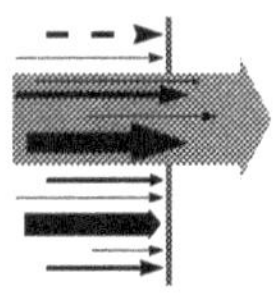

Figure 12. Force Box

Putting it all together

The art of living involves knowing how to identify and manage complexity to the extent that you can develop to your fullest potential. When you put these three graphic components together- the oval system, the balancing scale, and box- you can design strategies for problem solving and decision making. Figure 12 shows the strategy I used by implementing this method of problem identification and solving. After Figure 13, I have provided Senge's "how to" methods for detecting and dealing with limits to growth in your life. It puts all the elements together and can assist you when someone is trying to shift a burden of irresponsible activity to your shoulders.

Here's the strategy I used. It is placed in a systems perspective:

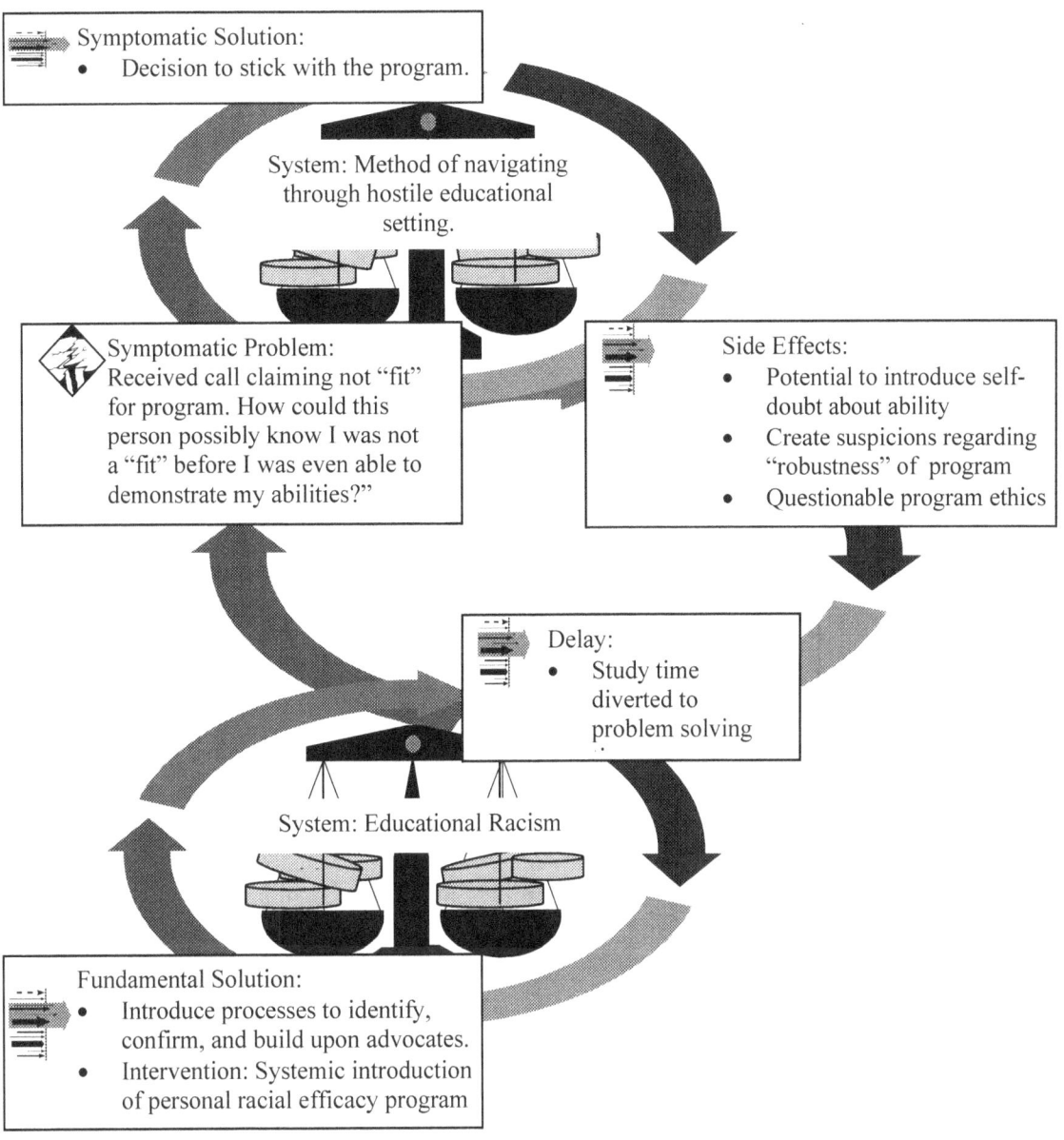

Figure 13. Identify and deal with symptomatic problems with fundamental solutions

Identify and deal with symptomatic problems appropriately. Understand that symptomatic solutions are designed to get your through the immediate situation. In the back of your mind, you should be building a framework for identifying the institutional conditions that generated the symptomatic problem. Identify the fundamental problem and design an arsenal of fundamental solutions, long term – strategies, for dealing with discriminatory practices you have identified and that are infused in the educational environment. Use Figure 13 as a template for identifying burdens that are unnecessarily shifted to your shoulders.

Shifting the Burden is an age-old phenomenon in African-American experience. The dominant white culture in America has always justified its bigotry by creating myths of African irresponsibility, intellectual weakness, and criminality. It is a method of blaming the victim and it diverts attention away from the real issues- the continued, sanctioned expression, enforcement, and perpetuation of racism in America. After years of experiencing a variety of deception techniques, I knew the department head's phone call was another manipulation tactic. As a person of color, I simply refused to buy-in to age-old arguments that imply Blacks are innately problematic. Students of color are not problematic… it is the thought processes of others that is problematic. I place the burden back where it was imagined and created.

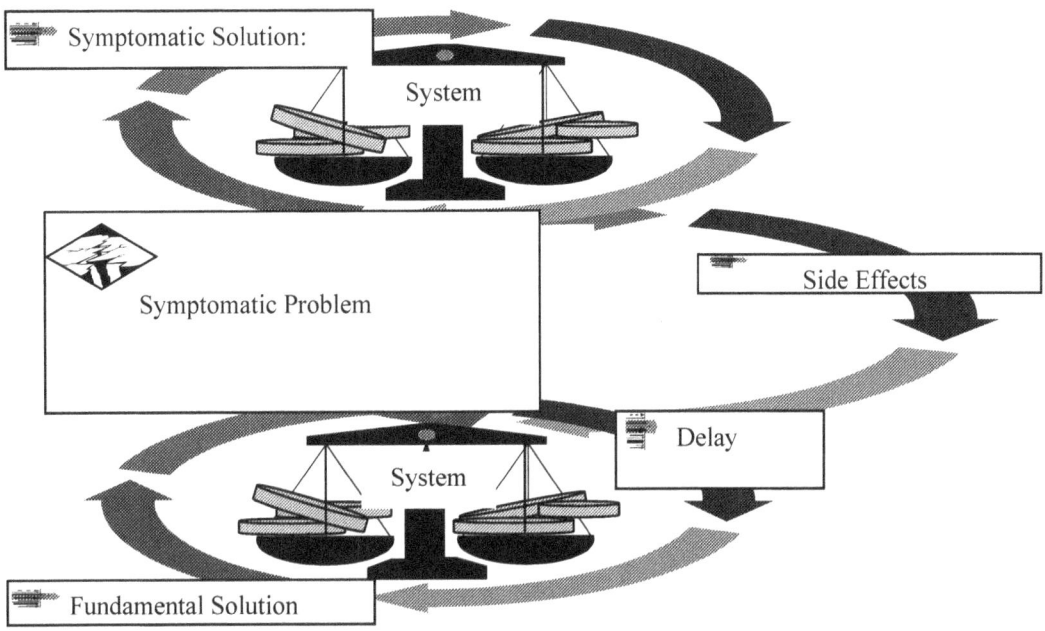

Figure 14. Students of Color: How To Create Your Own "Shifting The Burden Story"

Table 10

<u>Students of Color: How To Create Your Own "Shifting the Burden Story"</u>

Step	Action
1	IDENTIFY the problem symptom, the "squeaky wheel" in educational progress
2	IDENTIFY a "fundamental solution," a course of action for an enduring educational solution
3	IDENTIFY a "symptomatic solution," a temporary solution in educational experience
4	IDENTIFY the negative effects of the symptomatic solution
Insights	
• Distinguishing different types of solutions • Continual reliance on symptomatic solutions reinforces further reliance	
Leverage	
• Strengthen bottom circle, and/or • Weakening top circle • Test in small increments and allow time for results	
SOURCE: Adapted from – <u>The fifth discipline</u> (p. 113), by P. M. Senge, 1990, New York: Doubleday.	

Keeping Your Eyes Wide Open

Analyzing what is known in complex educational settings.

The first thing to remember about keeping your eyes open is that you can't see everything. When the student of color enters the educational environment, the development of sound interpersonal and group relationship skills can not be underestimated. One tool I have found helpful in understanding social interactions is the Johari Window (Natemeyer and Gilberg, 1989). This model helped me understand the complexity in human interactions. If you can't figure out what is going on in a particular situation, consider conducting the following analysis.

There are many levels of awareness in the human experience, and this model identifies these dynamics.

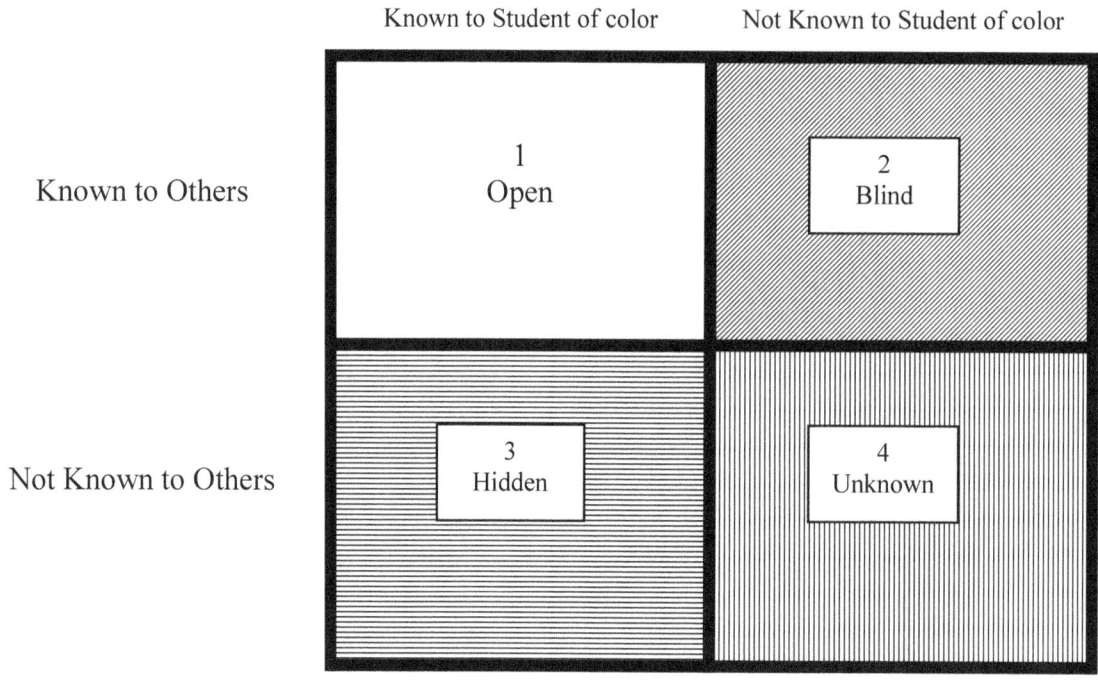

Figure 15. The Johari Window. SOURCE: Adapted from – <u>Classics of organizational behavior</u> (2nd ed.), (pp. 131-4), by H. Natemeyer &, J. Gilberg, 1989, Danville: Interstate.

Table 11

Student of Color Johari Quadrant Chart

Quadrant	Area Description
1	The area of free activity, or open area. This region refers to behavior and motivation known to the student of color and known to others.
2	The blind area. This is the region where others can see things in the student of color that the student of color is unaware.
3	The avoided or hidden area. This region represents things the student of color knows but does not reveal to others. This can be an area about which the student of color has sensitive feelings.
4	The area of the unknown. This is the region where neither the student of color nor others are aware of certain behaviors or motives. The student of color can assume the existence of these behaviors because eventually some of these things become known, and then the student of color realizes that there are unknown behaviors and motives that are influencing relationships all along.
SOURCE: Adapted from – Classics of organizational behavior (2nd ed.), (pp. 131-4), by H. Natemeyer &, J. Gilberg, 1989, Danville: Interstate.	

Innuendo: Learning to "Read Between the Lines"

Accurately interpreting and clarifying remarks that potentially debilitate.

I had just completed a graduation ceremony at one institution when a student came up to me and said, "Well, have you decided what you want to be when you grow up?" I took this to be a cloaked assumption that I was still considered a "child" in the eyes of the speaker. The remark sparked another strategy to be shared. This skill is essential on interpersonal, group, and institutional levels of social interaction. Learn to read between the lines of innuendo in the educational setting. Reading between the lines is a form of critical thinking that helps people work in the realm of the obscure, vague, unknown, and ignorant. Reading between the lines helps you understand and handle overt and covert meanings embedded in messages and agendas that have the potential to disrupt your educational experience, divert you from your purpose, or lead you into traps.

Quizzical remarks and statements made on the educational scene can be troublesome. These remarks can occur in social interactions, conversations with faculty and staff, or can emerge as comments on schoolwork. They can be dealt with in the following way. First, determine if these remarks are worth the time to dignify. This decision is based on whether or not these communications can in any manner block goals acquisition. If they do not block goal acquisition, drop it. If they do have an impact, design and employ an inquiry method that will allow you to arrive at the true meaning and intent of the remark. Let's briefly look at some methods.

Develop the ability of talking to others, receiving feedback from others, reading research, and reviewing graded work. In conversations and discussions relevant to your educational progress, ask for clarification if a message appears oblique, insulting, unclear, clouded, or mystical. Professionally question the overuse of jargon, and know that many people use it to conceal the fact that they do not know their subject matter. In graded materials returned to you, read comments carefully. If a vague comment is made regarding the quality of your work, and it is has a negative impact on your grade, ask for clarification if you feel the argument is not proven. Always ask for examples of appraiser expectations or further references that support the negative appraisal. Many times students accept a grade based on the positional power of the appraiser. Questionable or debatable feedback may be based on biased opinion and this can effect the equitable evaluation of your work. If you select to contest a grade, be prepared to defend your argument for the deserved grade with supporting information (the facts).

Always ask yourself what is being assumed in the communication process. Here is a very effective method I have used to get to the questionable intent of message, it also works in general situations where you want to analyze the stamina of a person's argument or cause. It reveals the ways in which the speaker can manipulate situations in order to avoid dealing with what is actually thought and felt. This diversionary method prevents a counterproductive situation from improving.

Table 12

Left-Hand Column Exercise

Step	Activity
1	DRAW a line down the center of a piece of paper.
2	WRITE out a sample script of the exchange on the right hand side.
3	WRITE what is thought but not said as each stage of the exchange on the left hand side.
SOURCE: Adapted from – The fifth discipline (p. 196), by P. M. Senge, 1990, New York: Doubleday.	

Use this exercise to bring hidden assumptions to light and show how they influence behavior in situations (Senge, 1990). Mentally assimilate this exercise as a tool for active critical listening, thinking and problem solving. For example, when I am listening to another person, I ask myself what is being thought but not said. It is a powerful way of uncovering the operating assumptions of the speaker and is a very effective way of "reading between the lines."

Developing X-Ray Vision

Understanding unseen relationships in educational settings.

"You like to have your cake and eat it too," said my graduate faculty advisor. These poisoned darts were thrown in my direction during an appraisal session in a graduate program. The small, dimly-lit room seemed to shrink around me and the hard florescent light above gave the advisor's face a grey, ghostly pallor. I sat there stunned, and allowed the silence in the room to call for an explanation. I remember sensing the pleasure in his voice, felt him feel his power as he delivered his condemning verdict. "There's been talk around the faculty, and that's what they say about you," he said.

I understood the original purpose of the meeting to be a review of academic progress, so I refocused on the task at hand. Yet, on the inside I felt broken-hearted, betrayed, blindsided, and misled by a tactic of institutional discouragement. I smiled, remarked that I found the information intriguing, and moved the meeting on to a review of my educational progress. As the interview continued, my fingers turned ice-cold, my face flushed. I realized that aside from academic performance, there were other evaluation criteria used to plot my progress. I wondered what those other evaluation criteria might be. My head got light as I realized that although I only knew a handful of professors, a web of communication channels existed within the department. I was unaware of it. I began to realize that the texture of these communications had the potential to assassinate my character.

I thought to myself, "Was it because of a recent field assignment request I placed?" It required a faculty member from this upper middle class conservative white institution to make a field visit to a lower class African - American site. It was my logical career choice as my career objective at the time was to work in the African – American community. I discovered later in another conversation with another advisor that the request appeared to present an unnerving situation for the department.

I believe in acquiring experiences that bring out your very best. I believe in educational program development that comprehensively meets the needs of its participants. For the program participants who embrace this philosophy, asking for what meets your needs may mean slightly pushing the educational envelope occasionally. Senge (1990) shows how this works in the concept of personal mastery. In this book, personal mastery can be seen as a way of using personal power for leverage in the accomplishment of goals. For example, each situation in life holds a creative tension. I represent this creative potential in the form of contending arrows. See Figure 16. In each situation, these arrows symbolize an amalgamation of forces that have the potential to either impede or advance your growth and development as an individual.

The way in which African Americans successfully navigate and rise through governmental and business hierarchy is an example of personal mastery. These individuals, I believe, have effectively used contending forces in their respective disciplines to rise to the highest levels the structure would allow. In short, as you go through life there are many contending forces that have the potential to impede or advance your growth and development as an individual. These forces, for example cultural norms, carry the potential to shape our occupational self-image and take the form of personal belief systems.

The African American has always had to master societal forces that exert a tension in the realization of their dreams. Where there is racial prejudice and discrimination a tension exists between personal and social goals. In the academic setting this is seen as the tension between the vision and the reality of achieving an advanced degree. The student of color must simultaneously pull the vision towards current reality and pull current reality towards the vision in order to "hold the tension" for getting the advanced degree, not get discouraged, and achieve the dream.

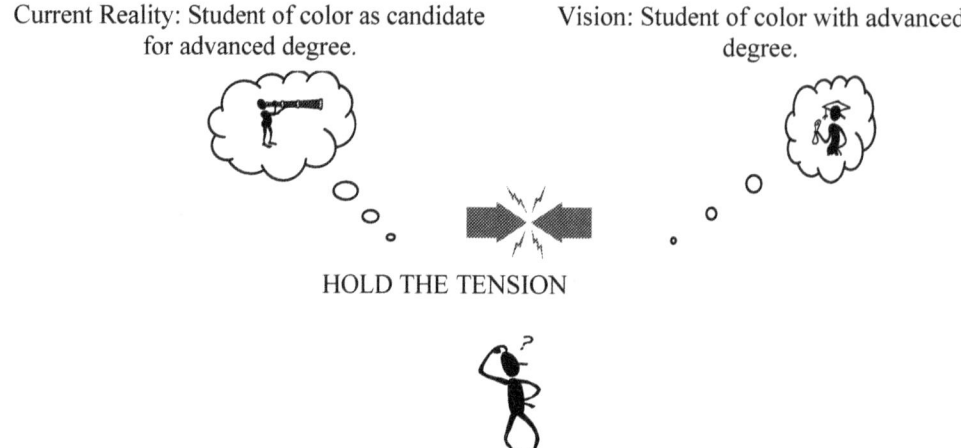

Figure 16. Student of Color: Holding Creative Tension

As I look back on the interview with the faculty advisor, my unique field request raised the ire of the faculty. The collective departmental discontent emerged at my academic review. The faculty advisor was the messenger and the message being delivered in the form of a dubious academic appraisal. It was a demonstration of illogical protest on an institutional level. The expression of displeasure took the form of an Ad hominem argument, that is, attacking a student during an academic review.

Judging a book by its cover had taken on a new meaning for me in a twinkle of an eye. This sole interview shifted my way of looking at faculty members. I refer to a model of figure/ground shifts- shifting one's view from objects to relationships, originating from the work of Capra (1996). It clearly explains the perceptual shift I experienced regarding faculty relationships.

Before the performance review, I saw faculty members as a group of independent experts who took the forefront in my educational development. I assumed that they had minimal contact with each other with respect to communications about my academic

character. See Figure 17.

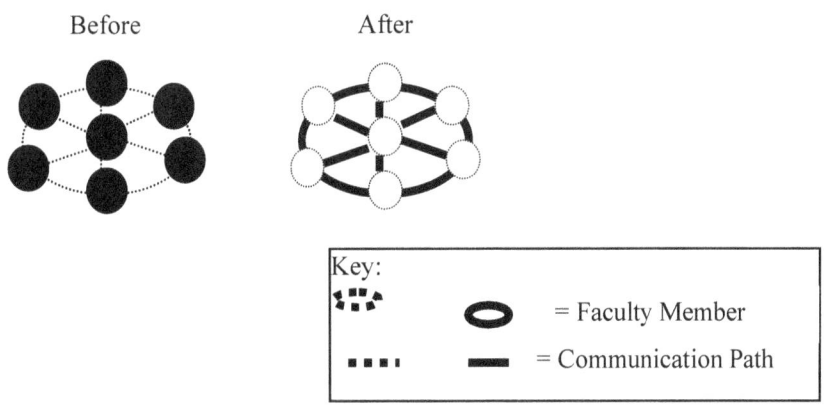

Figure 17. Overt and Covert Faculty Relations

After the performance review my conceptions about distinct faculty personas seemed

to fade into the mist as their communications about my academic character emerged out of

the mist. A new understanding about faculty interpersonal relationships took a multi-

dimensional form. On the level of the "seen," faculty members were regarded as individuals.

On the level of the "unseen" there existed a network of interactions and exchanges that took

on an anonymous texture (Capra, 1996).

One lesson learned from this account is to watch and see if you have been out-

grouped by the institution. For example, observe the quality and quantity of exchanges you

have with faculty. Consider if and how faculty interpersonal relations affect your progress as

a student. In my case and as a result of this incident, I began to develop relationships with

faculty members within the department that I felt had my best interests at heart. It was

through these wholesome relationships that I found a way to identify and navigate my way

through the territory of the unseen. On the observable level, I contacted the head of the department, who in-turn, stepped forward to be my field advisor. I was able to have a productive, appropriate field experience that matched my social reality as an African American in America. As I look back, I know that this was the time I began to develop x-ray vision.

Earning your degree with integrity

Grounding your learning on an identified set of personal values.

"I'll get you though the program, don't worry," the stranger said. Then he vanished into the crowd at the orientation session. He had taken me aside from a general body of program participants to make the clandestine remark. He was the dean of a graduate program I was interested in attending. His approach was somewhat unnerving on two levels. First, I felt he had some information about my academic potential that prompted the remark. Second, I felt it was an unethical. The event created a mild degree of self – doubt that replaced a fresh enthusiasm and made me wonder if there was a "twilight zone" to getting a degree, a hidden or unknown territory.

The dean's line of reasoning could be linked in part to a fallacy called "division." In short, if a whole is known to have a particular characteristic, then its parts must have the same characteristic as well. I perceived that the dean thought Blacks always had problems getting through this level of the educational system, therefore being Black, I would also have problems. I felt that I had a choice: to either leave the program or continue. I selected to continue with the program and my plan was simple. For each milestone of the program, I decided to get a thorough understanding of course of objectives. Then I decided to match my work, point for point, to each course objective. If this honest strategy did not work, then I would look for similar programs at other institutions and transfer.

I attribute my approach to my fundamental base of values and a clear sense of self. I know what I stand for and I wanted to walk into the world, and especially the Black community with a sound professional knowledge base. I attribute this to the way I was raised by my mother and the sound real world experiences relayed by my father. My values were galvanized into a strong system of beliefs. This prepared me for racial oppression in America. Strong networks of values and beliefs have always carried me through good and bad times.

When value bases have been established or reaffirmed, a personal method for making transitions into and within educational settings is in order. This means doing a little research before a discipline or course is selected. Take a little time to find out how the discipline or course fits into the master occupational plan. Compare this information with an identified base of values. See Table 13 for an idea of some things to ask before pursuing a new discipline or course.

Table 13

Student of Color Guide to Coming To Grips With A New Subject or Discipline

• How is this area of knowledge or practice developed and how does it fit in to my unique situation as a minority practitioner? • What are some of the basic concepts and terms and how do they fit in to my experience as a minority practitioner? • What are some of the key theories and how do they apply to my situation as a minority practitioner? • What are the most widely respected authorities and who respects them from an ethnic perspective? • What are one or two recommended primers and how do I as a minority practitioner respond to the information?
SOURCE: Adapted from – Learning how to learn: applied theory for adults (p. 124), by R. Smith, 1982, New York: Free Press.

Evaluate the usefulness of a course. Scrutinize it from every possible angle in terms of meeting your occupational needs. Ask if there is a clash with your fundamental base of values and beliefs. If there is a decision to enroll in a course, actively review the material received for its relevance to occupational and social reality. Build upon information that resonates internally and keep an open mind to all forms of new knowledge. Anytime institutional lines of reasoning that appear illogical or unclear, ask for clarification from informational resources. Request for clarification in a professional demeanor when there is confusion or vagueness. Table 14 gives a framework for collecting information.

In review, approach all claims for "fast track" advancement through an educational program with scrutiny. Put professional competency before anything else. Avoid succumbing to ever-present cultural forces suggest ethnic and racial inferiority and consequently educate in an inferior manner. Have a base of wholesome ethical values and operate from that base. Design a sound system of goal achievement on this foundation.

Table 14

Student of Color Guide to Assessing The Potential Usefulness of a Course

• Look for claims that sound excessive in relation to the amount of instructional time
• Look for specific information about the objectives and about the activities that will be used to achieve them
• See if the qualifications of the instructor are made clear
• Look for signs that provision will be made for feedback and evaluation
Once Enrolled, You are entitled to:
• A clear statement of what you are expected to know or be able to do upon completing the course and watch if expectations are lowered or raised in your case
• Information about the kind of preparation expected for sessions as opposed to what the instructor can be expected to provide and watch if the expectation are lowered or raised in your case • Opportunities to receive accurate feedback and question feedback reflects personal stereotypical bias or opinion
• The right to express values and points of view toward subject matter that differ from those of authorities and cautiously navigate situation that systematically hamper or contain you right to expression
SOURCE: Adapted from – Learning how to learn: applied theory for adults (p. 120), by R. Smith, 1982, New York: Free Press.

If the educational system does not respond to honest achievement, then:

1.   Exert creative tension to navigate through the setting, or

2.   Find another institution to complete studies.

In addition to conducting personal research, remember to find strength in relationship networks. Family, friends, and professional associates can provide strong models of determination and persistence. Models can also be found in ethnic history and are an essential part of a formula for success. Surround yourself with symbols of encouragement, inspiration, and success. On my desk I have a set of principles that are in a picture frame. Whenever I fall upon hard times, these principles have served as a source of inspiration to move forward. On my walls I have a variety of things the represent past achievements and these symbols have also encouraged me to move forward.

Know "Self" and have a strong network of support. This combination provides the perfect context for evaluation of a discipline, institution, and contents of a course. Self-knowledge facilitates the match of occupational goals to core values, allows proper self-assessment of educational needs, and helps determine if the educational pursuit truly meets those needs. With this in mind, we move to a discussion of educational reality.

Basing action on educational reality

Operating with others as a Student of Color in the educational setting.

To McClenney (1987):

… the language of white folks is such that communication takes place in ways we (Black folks) don't pick up. As applied in higher education, the signals of language are exclusive to the majority of people who run the school. (p. 45)

Consider using relevant points from McClenney's advice to Black folk:

Table 15

McClenney's Academic Terrorism- Implicit Classroom Norms for Black Folks

Remember this:	
1.	Get it set in your mind that the classroom is not a democratic setting.
2.	You want your education and diploma, that's all.
3.	To the fullest extent possible, learn to write white.
4.	Learn how to take tests, essay or multiple choice.
5.	Associate with your fellow white students.
6.	Arrange your financial affairs so that you do not have to work while studying full time.
SOURCE: Adapted from – How to survive when you're the only black in the office (p. 42), by E.H. McClenney, 1987, First Associates Publishing: Richmond Virginia.	

I encountered turbulence in my educational settings. In my case, the consistent challenge was to learn when I was being deceived. Then, I had to learn how to respond to these situations in a way that balanced the scales of fairness. The maneuver had to be conducted without eliciting reprisal from staff, faculty, administration, and fellow students. When turbulence is sensed in group settings, response should be based upon an understanding of environmental characteristics and social and political forces at large. Be equipped with the tools to respond to environmental forces that cause turbulence. Base responses on four principles. The tool below describes what to look for in order to define a turbulent learning situation and what principles are used in order to ensure responsive success.

Table 16

Active Adaptation To Turbulent Group Environments

Characteristics of Turbulent Environments	Active Adaptation Principles
Unexpected Changes	Flexibility
Uncertainty	Innovation/Creativity
Unintended Consequences	Social Responsibility
Complexity	Participation
Adaptation Principles	
Flexibility	
COME well – prepared to engage in activities being able to participate, and make decisions if appropriate.	
Innovation	
ENCOURAGE the generation of new ideas- use brainstorming, and through this exercise, distinguish original thought from value judgement in order to encourage change.	
Social Responsibility	
INFLUENCE group decisions. PROMOTE the scrutiny of potentially unethical suggestions if appropriate.	
Participation	
INCLUDE everyone who is affected or who affects the situation.	
SOURCE: Adapted from – Discovering common ground (p. 75), by M. Weisbord, 1992, Berrett-Koehler.	

Unsure about how a group operates? Create a mental framework for group behavior.

When working with others in collaborative learning settings, keep things in perspective by

having a plan, similar to the one shown in Table 17:

Table 17

Student of Color Guide to Successful Group Work

Step	Action
1	Identify a common interest or need of those who will participate.
2	Develop topics.
3	Set goals for the learning activity.
4	Select appropriate resources.
5	Select appropriate procedures or strategies.
6	Put the main activities into a format and time schedule.
SOURCE: Adapted from – Learning how to learn: applied theory for adults (p. 113), by R. Smith, 1982, New York: Free Press.	

Understand the social contracts in American race relations and how they manifest specific to group behavior in the educational setting. Consider "The Only One Syndrome" in the African American experience. A form of tokenism, many students of color actually get "energy" and "feel special" by being the only person of color in a group setting. In a culture where Blacks are essentially invisible, assuming a role that facilitates a degree of acknowledgement in an integrated setting is important. Yet many times I've observed that Blacks in integrated settings often default to either a subservient position in the group, become the group's caretaker, or succumb to some other culturally bound behavior. These images conjure stereotypes that prohibit full professional development and carry the potential to block the progress of other people of color. Although luscious to some students of color, resist the temptation to behave in stereotypical ways that advance a dysfunctional or inappropriate educational climate. Be yourself.

Chapter Summary

Understand that there could be psychological race warfare in a white graduate school program. As a student of color, this behooves total connection to "Self" by constantly monitoring mental and emotional constitutions. Be constantly vigilant for environmental forces of deception and distraction- they delay progress. Students of color must contend with many internal and external forces in addition to the responsibilities of being a student. They must have a way of analyzing this complexity. Diversionary tactics that delay may come in the form of wise cracks or other ambiguous communication. Interpret these communications for their ability to cause psychological, intellectual, and emotional damage. Formulate ways to protect yourself in these areas.

Remember that there is an unseen side to organizational dynamics in educational settings. Consider these forces if a received grade or appraisal appears to be questionable. Create a personal master plan of problem solving as a roadmap in such settings. Fold in a heavy component of collaborative learning. This helps to add different perspectives to your educational experiences. Identify and/or create an ethical base of fundamental values and act from that base. Acknowledge the forces that affect students for color in an educational setting and use these forces as leverage. There is a condition of racial and ethnic warfare in many of America's educational institutions. Prepare yourself for the possibility of doing battle. Having established a possible context for your educational experience, we now move to additional tools used to master the situation.

YOU CAN AND MUST SUCCEED, HERE IS WHY

Introduction

This chapter opens by introducing why and how the student of color can and must succeed in a racially hostile educational environment. Some strategies, in the form of text, charts and tables, are provided as tools for enabling the student to re-define their success in realistic terms as a student of color in a graduate institution.

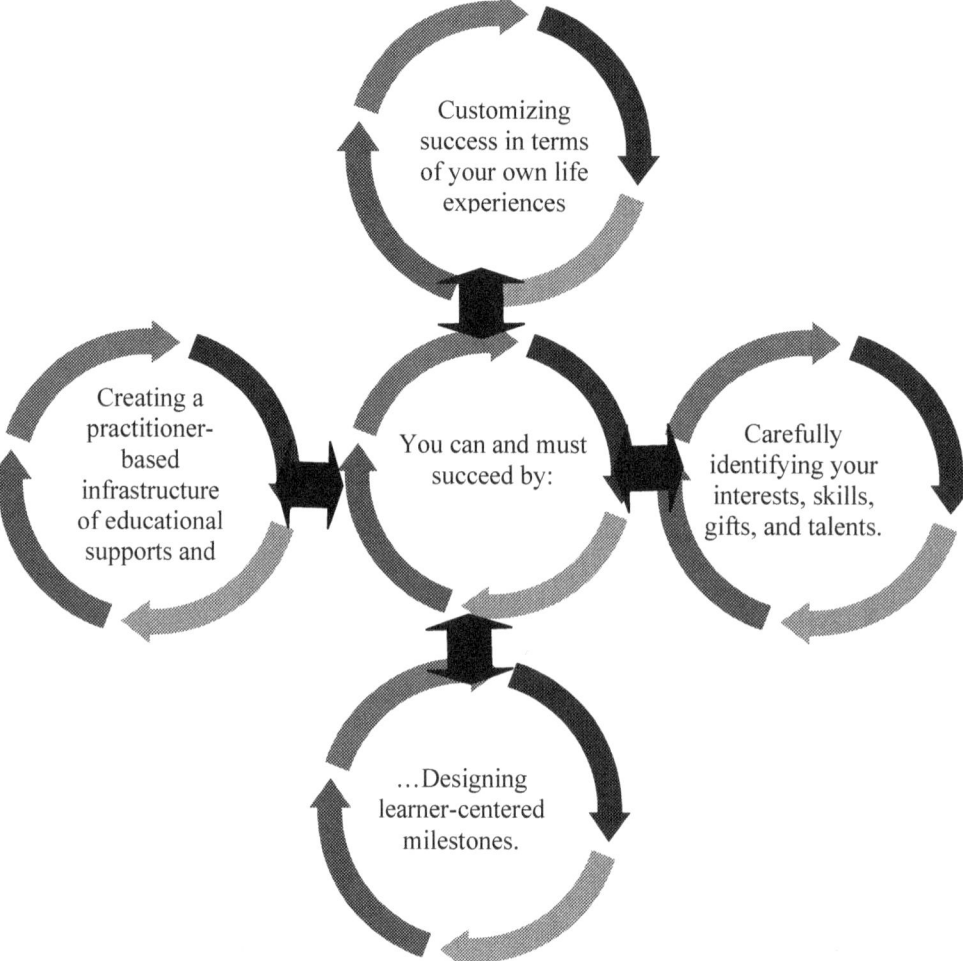

Figure 18. Orchestrated Leadership: You Can and Must Succeed

Following this line of logic, the student of color is shown how to develop an educational action plan geared to specific skills, gifts, talents, and abilities. This chapter continues with a strategy that allows the creation of milestones in a learner - centered environment using an action plan as a means for plotting learner progress. The chapter concludes stressing the importance of human networks. Figure 18 illustrates how Orchestrated Leadership is used to organize essential elements of student success. First, we examine the process of defining your own reality.

Creating Your Own Bar of Success

Customizing success in terms of your own life experiences.

"Success" is a relative term. In this society, "success" is often couched in terms of leading big companies, important titles, and lots of money. For many Blacks who are barred from many visual opportunities, the American Dream becomes the Impossible Dream. Yet, People of Color, especially Blacks, succeed through determination and persistence. For the student of color, it is important to understand that success can occur in such conditions, however, compare personal, intellectual, and spiritual worth against an educational criterion built in the context of cultural reality. For skeptics who believe the educational reality is the same for all individuals, I submit the raging legal battles over Affirmative Action in American institutions of higher learning for consideration. As we enter the 21st century, these battles tell People of Color that they must be resourceful in obtaining their educational goals and success.

Creating a personal bar of educational success is important for many reasons. First, understand that in the larger social context, being a success in American society is largely dependent upon an Euro - centric model, which includes white skin color. This fundamental criterion automatically excludes the person of color, no matter how hard they try to assimilate. In order to succeed in this kind of environment, people of color usually find themselves emulating behaviors labeled as "acceptably Euro – centric" in order to "fit – in" and "get ahead." People of color will never truly succeed in a race – based white structure because they lack THE essential ingredient, they are not white. The student of color must base success on a supportive environment that reflects the cultural reality of living in a covertly racist society.

Second, creating a personal bar of success means understanding the "perfect deception" inherent in fundamentally racist educational systems. Racism is equipped with a component of "tokenism" that allows a few People of Color to be visually present in many American educational positions. Racist educational systems do this in order to counter claims of bigotry. A graduate school that appears culturally diverse does not necessarily mean that the racial personality of the institution is "safe" and that the student of color will be successful. Success in subversive, racially hostile, educational environments is not based exclusively on talent and ability, race plays a big role. Given this situation, the student of color entrapped in an educationally hostile system essentially has two choices:

1.)   Succeed in the educational illusion at the price of losing self-identity.

2.)   Succeed in the educational illusion by creating your own educational reality, opportunities, and identity.

Third: a personal bar of success means understanding that there is no direct correlation between great talent and success in a latently racist graduate institution. For example, you may encounter faculty who may not have the need to be professionally robust in their interactions with students of color. In my experience, I have received marginal services from such individuals. This is why graduate students should respectfully challenge information when it does not resonate with their knowledge base. Be fully informed when you leave the graduate institution as a successful professional.

To many talented students of color, being admitted to a graduate institution is a great accomplishment. However, creating educational success after admission means pushing the envelope of resourcefulness. This involves the use of expert interpersonal communication skills and abilities. These skills and abilities contend with complex casual forces that have the potential to delay educational progress. The honest discussion for the student of color is whether or not they are willing to accept educational success in new networked dimensions in terms of time and space. Let me explain.

In terms of time, look at personal educational success from the perspective of previous experience in covert oppressive environments. In terms of space, identify how you have succeeded in such situations, and under what circumstances. Ask: What kind of working relationship was formed that enabled the success? This self-examination will result in a mental criterion of success techniques to be modified for the educational setting. Write these ways of knowing down and make them into a set of guiding principles. Post them in your work area. Building and comparing personal, intellectual, and spiritual worth against a self-designed educational criterion based on your cultural reality provides a clear window for educational success. We now move to a discussion on how to isolate and implement this set of self-defined criterion.

It's Your Party

Carefully identifying your interests, skills, gifts, and talents.

Shift the paradigm of success by carefully confirming your interests, skills, gifts, and talents. Link these attributes to how they have helped you achieve past success. Why? This author's past experience has shown that students of color will be tested on many levels and *need* to rely upon your success strategies. When going to get an advanced degree, reconfirm personal achievement skills to re-validate and buttress self- image and esteem. If the student of color is getting an advanced degree to enrich jobs skills, improve opportunities for advancement, or decide to create your own occupational reality, these achievement skills translate into transferable job skills. As stated in the previous section, be prepared to go out to compete in a hostile educational environment, be equipped with a sound set of proven success skills that have facilitated previous goal acquisition. Use the following chart to create a "pool" of proven success skills.

Table 18

Student of Color Achievement Worksheet for Skill Identification

Instructions:	I. Think of three past achievements.		
	II. List them here:		
	A.		
	B.		
	C.		
	III. Check the terms below that describe the skills used in your achievements. *Terms can be checked more than once.*		
4	**Skill**	**4**	**Skill**
	Direct		Investigate
	Report		Brief
	Govern		Collaborate
	Adapt		Compose
	Resolve		Generate
	Arrange		Estimate
	Pursue		Vision
	Conceive		Resourceful
	Produce		Devise
	Guide		Accomplish
	Attentive		Cautious
	Inspire		Encourage
	Mindful		Methodical
	Mobilize		Discern
	Insistence		Influence
	Convince		Strategic
	Accurate		Enterprise
	Predict		Cultivate
	Inquire		Display
	Articulate		Deliberate
	Sensitive		Educate
	Command		Impart
	Publish		Detail
List:	IV. Checked items are your constellation of achievement skills. Place the most frequently checked skills here		
Summarize on a separate sheet of paper:	V. How can these skills be applied towards your educational achievement?		

I had just finished getting an advanced degree after years of formal and informal institutionally sanctioned separation from a white student body. The separation was performed in an exquisitely simple, informal manner: people simply didn't communicate with me. Phone calls were not returned, nor was my correspondence answered. To my amazement, one day a student called my home after I graduated. She wanted to have dinner. I featured she was a "scout" sent out from the larger community. On the night of the dinner she wanted to understand, given the amount of racial anger she had seen at the school, how on earth I got through the program. I simply had not been invited to the party, she didn't understand.

"It's common knowledge," the student said at my dinner table. "I'm invited to the party and you are not. I [as a white person] *know* I don't have to do as much as you do to get my degree." I took a large drink of wine, looked at the student, said "Oh really?" In the back of my mind I wondered how many ill-prepared people there were in America who earned their degrees in the same manner.

One nugget of fallacious logic I detected in this student's line of thinking was that to be academically successful, you had to be part of the "in crowd." Her remarks contained underpinnings of "in-groups" and "out-groups." Her views conveyed the notion of privilege granted by institutional invitation. In my view, her line of reasoning was based on a real and very dangerous form of argument: false analogy. In this case, "in-group" status equated to educational and professional acceptance and success. Now, this student viewed herself as reasonably "politically correct:" a vogue term used at the time of this writing to describe the socially informed white person. In the final analysis she confided that the primary admission requirement to the party was race-based. Guess what race.

I explained to this person that I had already created by own party. Given my social situation, educational goals, and value base, I selected to go the road primarily on my own merit and with support from selected friends and family. I knew what was truly important to me. This self-knowledge drove the kinds of decisions I made with regard to my education. I had also decided to give it my best, know my subject well, and this led an emotional and psychological freedom from trying to "impress" or manipulate others- a popular phenomenon I observed in the educational institution. Weisbord (1992) provides a set of principles in his discussion of personal mastery. It captures the spirit of my sentiments on personal development.

Table 19

<u>Principles of Personal Mastery and Enrollment</u>

Identify what is truly important to you
Make a choice (commitment)
Be truthful with those around you regarding your choice
Do not try to manipulate others into agreement or superficial support
SOURCE: SOURCE: Adapted from – <u>Discovering common ground</u> (p. 310), by M. Weisbord, 1992, Berrett-Koehler.

I explained to the student that getting through the school was just one of the steps in a master plan that allowed me to realize professional potentials. Having this perspective helped to minimize the social exclusion that occurred on the educational level. It was important to me that I got a good education because of skills I wanted to share with the Black community. My primary needs were not focused on the social aspects of the institution, they were focused on the social aspects of being Black in America. I saw how my dinner guest framed the learning community as a social event, consequently, I understood how my dinner guest framed the process of academic achievement in the context of being "invited to the party."

I told her that helping others was important to me. So I made a choice to work in the area of human services. I felt that more needed to be done in professional communities about portraying Blacks in an accurate light. Creating the opportunity to excel intellectually and abandoning cultural notions that dictated who I was (and was not) drove my vision. It is from this initial vision that I crafted my personal path for career-development. This is a process of self-exploration and self-examination. It is the continuation of a life-long process involving personal learning and change.

It is *always* a very special time in life. To the person of color, experience as a whole individual is essential. Complete experience of humanness is tantamount in a society geared to systematically degrade and erase the true experience of people of color. In response, people of color must create activities designed to nurture the mind, body and spirit. In my experience, development of self-knowledge is instrumental in decision making. Ability to tap into strengths, gifts, and skills enables selection of what to study on the graduate level. This also results in the creation of productive relationships on personal, social, and professional levels. These connections facilitate personal growth and expression of personal talent. I have found, out of these relationships, the desire to help others is increased. Selfless service in these relationships increases spiritual awareness. Smith (1982), in his discussion on adult learning provides a framework for realizing new opportunities in life. It is holistic, meaning change occurs on many levels of human experience for the individual.

Table 20

Deciding What To Do

Concept	Description
Knowing thyself: Experiencing your mind and body	Activities that provide insight into one's behavior, body states, and feelings. May involve learning to control anger, tension or becoming more assertive.
Exploring the major fields of knowledge	The major subject matter fields associated with learning in schools and colleges.
Deepening personal relationships	The arts of friendship, intimacy, and love. Including parenting.
Learning how to help others to a better life	Learning for increased effectiveness in problem solving, community service, and social action.
Focusing on religious and spiritual growth	Learning related to a faith one already embraces.
SOURCE: Adapted from – <u>Learning how to learn: applied theory for adults</u> (p. 65), by R. Smith, 1982, New York: Free Press.	

Upon reflection, I now realize that these concepts are actually qualities. When coupled with a vision, these qualities crystallize into goal-directed behaviors and activities. In my case, I had to be *willing* to embark upon the journey and enroll my *abilities* to achieve my goals. As I took the necessary steps to reach my goals, I automatically began to look for models of leadership in my life. These role models served as examples of success. In turn, I began to realize that I became an example of leadership for others. Gradually I noticed a change in the way I formed ideas about the world. Instead of just accepting things as they stood, I began to question my reality. In order to find answers, I developed the ability to express my thoughts and feelings a clear and concise manner in a variety of different venues.

Develop the ability to direct personal learning in life. Remember that this is a life-long process so always maintain a curiosity about life. Cultivate the skill of asking career-based questions that are driven by your interests. Seek ways of finding out about occupational experiences. Explore ways of arriving at answers in achieving your prioritized goals. Consult with experts in the fields in which you are interested. Collect and study additional technical information from various sources, for example trade magazines and research. These kinds of activities can enable you to arrive at your own educational understandings. And above all remember: it's your party.

Developing the Educational Self

Designing learner-centered milestones.

Here are some elements to consider when developing your educational self and designing a personal program for goal acquisition.

Table 21.

Elements That Often Appear In Program – Planning Models	
Step	Action
1.	Determine needs and interests.
2.	Set goals and evaluation criteria.
3.	Identify promising resources and procedures.
4.	Select program format and activities.
5.	Conduct your program.
6.	Evaluate your outcome and conduct follow-up where appropriate.
SOURCE: Adapted from – Learning how to learn: applied theory for adults (p. 75), by R. Smith, 1982, New York: Free Press.	

I designed a personal plan for learning to achieve my educational goals. It was a powerful exercise because it taught me the importance of having a clear self – concept. I could gauge the accuracy of my self – concept by the degrees of success I experienced on my educational journey. One way of beginning of the educational journey, is to view it as a series of milestones. Then, reframe these milestones into a series of projects. From this perspective, design a project plan for accomplishing each milestone. First decide what to learn, then follow the subsequent steps in the checklist shown below. At the end of the process, conduct a self-evaluation with the checklist in order to improve your study, problem solving, and decision-making skills.

Table 22

Project Sheet: Checklist for Self-Directed Learning

Project:	Date Completed		
Activity	Need for Improvement Next Time		
	Little	Some	Much
1. Determine what to learn.			
2. Clarify goals and purposes.			
3. Specifying evaluative criterion.			
4. Identifying resources.			
5. Appraising the usefulness of resources.			
6. Deciding when to seek help.			
7. Choosing strategies.			
8. Execution of strategies:			
a. Interviewing and questioning			
b. Reading			
c. Listening			
d. Observing			
e. Viewing			
f. Practicing a skill			
g. Obtaining feedback			
h. Devising ways around blocks			
i. Creating suitable learning environment			
j. Applying what I learn			
k. Other			
9. Did the decision to carry out this project prove to be sound one?	Yes	No	N/A
10. What one or two insights were gained as a result of experience?			
SOURCE: Adapted from – Learning how to learn: applied theory for adults (p. 95), by R. Smith, 1982, New York: Free Press.			

For those who wish to use a less structured format, conduct the following self – analysis for development in these areas, use the following approach.

Table 23

Self-Analysis- Steps for Identifying Training and Educational Needs	
Step	**Action**
1.	EXAMINE Occupational Skill Requirements
	a. DETERMINE the skill requirements of the occupation.
	b. PRIORITIZE these skills in terms of:
	Physical requirements Mental requirements Emotional requirements
2.	EXAMINE Personal Skill for the Occupation
	a. COMPARE your present performance against the physical, mental, and emotional skill requirements of the occupation
	b. LOCATE the gaps between your performance and the skill requirements for the occupation.
	DETERMINE your developmental needs.
3.	PLAN Training and Development
	a. SET training and educational priorities
	b. DETERMINE required resources
	DISCOVER what resources: Are Available Need to be developed Need to be required
	Refer to this information when evaluating education programs of institutions.

At this point, validate findings. Reflect on the educational and training needs identified in the previous activity. Do these needs still match your original skills, talents, and ability and passion? If interests and occupational skill requirements are not in synch: 1.) Revisit interests, study them carefully, and see if occupational requirements are signaling true interests. 2.) Revisit occupational requirements, review them, and see if in some way these requirements need to be adjusted. 3.) Design an occupational plan to meet interests.

Engaging the Educational Self

Creating a practitioner-based infrastructure of educational supports and resources.

The holistic approach to educating the graduate degree student of color allows for the cultural inclusion of multiple support groups. Discover what resources are essential to increasing your probabilities of success. How can probabilities of success be increased given present resources? Design a systematic plan for including multiple resources as needed similar to the matrix shown below:

Table 24.

Student of Color Strategy For Building a Support Structure		
Resource	Steps of Inclusion To Take	Completion Date
Family		
Friends		
Work		
Professional		
Religious/Spiritual		
Literature		
Other Resources		

Be surrounded in a very supportive, positive environment. This should be done for each step of the action plan. Establish and develop relationships and contacts that have your best interests at heart. Also, develop an understanding of how various influences that can impede progress. Invite people to provide as many perspectives as possible during each step so you can make informed decisions.

View this experience in terms developing influential contacts in two different kinds of groups: functional groups and logical groups. Departments in an organizational hierarchy define functional groups. Logical groups are formed in order to reach goals and span across different functional groups within an organization. The influential collection of contacts developed across functional and logical groups are called linking pins and they are instrumental in facilitating your preparation for work. (O. Mink, Esterhuysen, B. Mink, Owen, 1993)

Data Collection from Resources

On the level of interacting with contacts, the graduate student of color must be very clear in purpose and deed. It helps to write things down and this keeps the individual in the present and provides data for reflective activity afterwards. Be sensitive to the very fact that there may be communication problems, not everyone sees the world in the same way as students of color do... students of color become "bicultural" at this stage of intellectual development. Remember that there will be forces that, as a student of color, must be shouldered alone and this is in addition to satisfying standard course requirements. Be prepared to encounter others who simply have no idea or could care less about this phenomenon.

Consult written materials, professionals, friends and family in this process. Understand that some resources will stay throughout the educational journey, while other resources may fall away entirely or reappear again as goals are approached. Below are some benefits and disadvantages of data collection:

Table 25

Student of Color Guide: Mink's Comparison Of Data Collection Techniques

Collection Method	Advantages	Disadvantages
Survey and questionnaires	More efficient for gathering perceptual data from large groups of people.	May not be specific enough to address all important concerns.
Interviews	Provide more in-depth information and richer descriptions of experiences.	Are limited to relatively small samples, so may not be representative of an organization or group of people as a whole.
Group Discussions	Enable people to share viewpoints and arrive at a consensus.	Require alot of time. May lead to limited sharing if group processes are inadequate.
SOURCE: Adapted from –Change at work: a comprehensive management process for transforming organizations (p. 178), by Mink, et.al., 1993, San Francisco: Jossey-Bass.		

When working with resources, step in their shoes and show sincere appreciation for having the privilege of meeting with them. Handle your interactions in a professional, relaxed manner using the same demeanor as in a business relationship. Be efficient, ask for clarification, and use positive reinforcement to keep the exchange going. Here are some guidelines for learning from a resource person:

Table 26

<u>Student of Color Guide: Learning From A Resource Person</u>

Planning	
Step	Action
1	CLARIFY what you want to learn. WRITE it down.
2	ANTICIPATE communication problems as a student of color.
3	CONSIDER environmental factors as a student of color.
4	PUT yourself in the resource person's place. What's in it for him or her as they communicate with a student of color?
5.	ORIENT the research person ahead of time.
During the Meetings	
Step	Action
1	MAKE your interests and objectives clear: "I want to learn enough of the technical vocabulary of investing to understand advice of professional advisers and brokers." "I'd like to be able to play well enough to enjoy the game by the end of the summer."
2	BE moderately assertive: "I afraid I don't follow that? Could you give me an example?" "Would you show me again more slowly? May I try it now?" "May I try to summarize?"
3	GIVE and SEEK feedback: "That's very helpful." "Am I asking the right questions?" "What do you think I ought to know next?" "I'm further along than I expected." "To be honest, that's more than I care to know about penguins."
SOURCE: Adapted from – <u>Learning how to learn: applied theory for adults</u> (p. 175), by R. Smith, 1982, New York: Free Press.	

In terms of identifying human resources, and organizing them into meaningful groupings, fold them into an educational identity. When meeting with individuals, treat them with respect, in a professional manner. This includes having clear communication skills. The professional contacts made during development of the educational self can make lifelong and enduring contacts. Treat them with care.

Effective planning in the development of your educational self is important. This book stresses that there is a link in the way you learn in life and what you want to do in life. Identify what you want to do and identify available resources necessary for reaching your goal. Design a program with milestones, and conduct and self – evaluation when each milestone has been reached. Ask yourself what you did right and what could have been done better. Fold these insights into the next leg of your journey.

Chapter Summary

When the person of color defines their success in terms of a Euro – centric standard of success, the probabilities of failure and disappointment increase. If not monetarily, a price is paid on mental and emotional levels. Define success based on a sound sense of social identity. This sense of identity is established on a personal knowledge of success skills. Conduct a self-analysis to know visible and invisible talents, skills, and abilities. Consider this an act of self-determination that launches and crystallizes self-actualization. Connect identified qualities to corresponding careers. Reflecting on what has been done in the past, and identifying those activities that "keep calling you back," is a good way of looking matching interests to careers.

For the person of color these activities are conducted in the context of overt and covert forces that have the capacity to delay, and possibly block the accomplishment of academic goals. Identification and development of the educational self occurs within these currents and it is a life-long enterprise. Prepare yourself- emotionally and mentally- for successes, failures, and delays. Yet remain focused, determined, and one-pointed: have a dream and reach the dream. When a vision has crystallized, apply it to occupational opportunities and industrial trends as they relate to people of color. This book is based on the assumption that anybody can do anything. However people of color will encounter social forces white people do not have to consider. Given this assumption, people of color are encouraged to pursue any occupation they wish with the understanding that they *may* take a little longer and worker a little harder to reach their dream. That is why it is important to set goals for achievement based on a personal set of circumstances. Remember, basing a timeline of success in terms of the white experience increases the possibilities for experiencing unnecessary disappointment. Be kind and patient to yourself with respect to these circumstances.

SUMMARY

SO YOU WANT AN ADVANCED DEGREE?!? One of the primary goals of this book was to orchestrate a multi-level discussion that addressed the numerous challenges students of color encountered in the American education school system. Personal thoughts and experiences from Dr. C.J.H. Dorsey and Dr. Frank Czarny were shared. Collectively, they felt the need to provide supplementary information on this subject, based on their personal and professional past.

Chapter I, *Understanding the relationship between race and advanced degrees,* provided a rationale for the need of more students of color to obtain advanced degrees. This chapter established the conversational stage for an in-depth historical accounting of events that formed some of the embedded educational challenges for so many African Americans. Other students of color may have encountered similar experiences.

Chapter II, *Engaging in institutional warfare and winning,* galvanized several issues and provided strategies for navigating institutional obstacles. The chapter provided guidance in the theatre of mental warfare for getting an advanced degree. The ideas and concepts presented in this chapter may be thought of as core measures, guiding your thinking and ways of being.

Chapter III, *You can and must succeed, here is why,* goes directly to the bottom line. This chapter may be considered as the discussion of motivation in this book. The previous chapters presented history, rationale and reasoning. Chapter III invites you to look, think, and act deliberately in order to achieve the ultimate goal.

Take a systematic approach to achieving your dreams. Base this approach on your set of ethical standards. Use the diagrams in this book as tools of analysis in the process of critical thinking and decision making. These tools will help you discern hidden and unseen forces that may inhibit your progress. These tools will help to understand that you have several choices in life, and that these choices can be prioritized into an effective plan for diversified personal learning and career development.

Constantly conduct self-checks by comparing contemporary activities with your original personal plans for learning. Adjust activities, or the plan, accordingly. Use a comprehensive system of identifying learning and occupational resources so you can get the big picture. The big picture shows the journey you need to take to reach your horizons. Your comprehensive system must include an infrastructure of support systems that facilitate your progress, cushion disappointments, and celebrate achievements. Develop a way of getting the information you need to ensure your achievements. Always treat these resources with respect, as these resources may be able to open alternative doors of opportunity when traditional doors are closed.

JOURNAL AND NOTATION DIARY

Significant Notable Events (SNE)

Introduction

The purpose of the SNE is to assist in developing and maintaining a dairy of significant events. All too often overt and covert discriminatory acts occur and go unaddressed. It is imperative to keep notes on subtle acts of oppression. The questions, "What do you know, when did you know it, and who knows about it?" is extremely relevant in terms of problem identification and resolution. The journal approach allows you to develop an internal dialog with the Educational Self. It is a dynamic record and you will add, remove, and contemplate its contents. It reflects your lived experience, which is dynamic. Very careful study of the contents results in new perspectives, insights, revelations, and awareness to aid in the successful completion of your journey. It is a profound tool and a suggested format for documentation follows.

What happened?_____

_____

When did it happen? (Date)_____

Where did it happen?_____

_____

_____

Who was involved?_____

_____

_____

Who did you tell? (Witnesses)_____

_____

_____

Additional Notations:_____

_____

_____

QUICK START: COMMUNITY - BASED GROUP APPROACH

The section is built upon bringing private and hidden discriminatory forces out into the open for group strategic development. Group dialog is one way of allowing this process to occur. In a group setting, participants can resort to a multiplicity of perspectives to clearly identify problems and create action plans that remove barriers to degree acquisition. The only qualification for starting a group is a genuine and sincere desire to succeed in an ethical manner. Although not a requirement, consider having an organization (i.e. club, church, or business) sponsor the group. The sponsorship approach opens the door to numerous sponsor resources.

Set group norms before beginning. Have group members agree to meet on a continuous basis, over a long period of time. This enables bonding to occur within the group and allows for the expression of deep trials and tribulations. Also, strong personal friendships occur in such situations. To this end, encourage a supportive, unconditional environment of inclusion. This means looking past insignificant idiosyncrasies and requiring complete agreement to do so from the group.

When interacting in the group, focus on your personal experiences and issues. Observations and information, collected through the interviews and journaling procedures suggested in this book, is brought to the table. Allow the group to examine emergent issues culled from your observations and experiences. In this way the group can analyze relationships between personal and institutional issues. Strategies and action plan arise from such discussions. Results of these discussions can again be noted in a personal journal for an: 1.) internal problem-solving dialogue with yourself; 2.) self-assessment and evaluation; 3.) strategic planning and implementation.

This section is based on the premise that *group* problem identification and resolution is a learned skill. To this end, exercises are provided to enable groups to hone their collective problem solving skills. These exercises can be used as ice breakers, be regular part of group meetings, be revisited over time for comparative purposes.

History – *Knowing where you've been provides a foundation for where you're going.*

Exercise 1.1: Exploring Significant Life Events

1. Ask each group participant, "What two significant life events led to the decision to obtain an advanced degree?" Each participant should write down a two sentence response.

2. Ask the participants to compare answers. Are they the same, are they different? Discuss.

Exercise 1.2: Familial Experiences

1. Ask each group participant to discuss their family's personal experiences with American, or other, educational systems. Allow each participant to share at least two experiences, good, bad, or neutral.

2. While each person is speaking, instruct listeners to jot down points that converge or diverge from personal family experiences.

3. Have a group discussion on notes that emerge from the exercise, looking for common themes as well as remarkable differences.

<u>Understanding the Relationship Between Race and Advanced Degrees</u> – *How belief systems*

perpetuate institutional racism.

Exercise 2.1: Exploring Institutionalized Race-Based Learning Theory

1. Ask each group participant to examine Figure 3, "The Myth of African American Inferiority," and draw a similar diagram representing personal perspectives regarding educational system under examination.

2. Ask each student to share their individual diagrams.

3. Conduct a large group discussion creating a group diagram which reflects the group sentiment. Revisit diagram and modify frequently over time.

Exercise 2.2: Examining Institutional Claims of Racial Parity

1. Ask the group to review Table 1, "Profiling Institutional Racial Parity Theories." Discuss the difference between espoused theory and theory-in-use.

2. Conduct a large group discussion based on the "Some questions to ask" section in Table 1. Encourage group participants to provide real-world examples to support claims and assertions.

3. Conduct and implement an action plan session based on group outcomes.

Exercise 2.3: Operational Definition: Institutional Personality Clash

1. Ask the group to review, Table 2, "Strength in Numbers." Have participants come up with a group definition to the following question: "What does it mean to have a personality clash with an institution?"

2. Ask participants to write down real and possible personality clashes with an institution, based

3. Conduct a large group session to create a group operational definition of a an institutional personality clash group. (Tip: focus on personal norms, values and beliefs versus real and perceived institutional norms, values, and beliefs.)

4. Conduct a problem solving session allowing the group to address any real, perceived, or potential participant personality clashes. Plan accordingly.

Exercise 2.4: Academic Terrorism

(Tip: This exercise can be assigned at the *end* of a group meeting, allowing participants to conduct field research. Results are discussed at the next meeting.)

1. Have participants review Table 4, "McKenney's Academic Terriorism: Exploring the Depth of an Institution's Racial Personality."

2. Assign each research question to group participants for data collection.

3. Send the participants into the field to collect data.

4. Re-assemble group, tabulate participant findings, both qualitative and quantitative.

5. Conduct in-depth discussion.

Exercise 2.5: Graduate Schools and Five Characteristics for Students of Colors to Consider

1. Have participants review Table 5, "Graduate Schools and Five Characteristics for Students of Colors to Consider."

2. Individually or in pairs, evaluate the institution under study according to the five dimensions of the table.

3. Come together in a large group to discuss appraisals and summarize findings.

Exercise 2.6: The Student of Color, Deciding the Future

1. Have participants look at Table 6, "The Student of Color, Deciding the Future." Then have each participant write down a response to each question in the table.

2. Then, review and discuss Figure 4, "Current Reality and Students of Color." Have each student create a diagram similar to Figure 4 using the responses provided for Table 6.

3. Conduct a large group discussion having each participant discuss their diagram.

Exercise 2.7: Predicting Changes in the Environment of the Student of Color

1. Have each participant complete the activity given in Table 7. (Suggestion: Allow at least 1 hour for this.)

2. In dyads or triads have participants present, discuss, and revise their predictions.

3. Have participants come together in large group to discuss insights and awareness gained from completing the activity.

Exercise 2.8: Force Field Analysis for Goal Acquisition

1. Direct each participant to review Figure 5, "Force Field Analysis," and its set of instructions.

2. Have each student create their own force field analysis according to these instructions.

3. Allow participants to present their diagram to the group for discussion and analysis.

<u>Engaging Institutional Mental Warfare and Winning</u> – *Using tactics in a subtle race war*

Exercise 3.1: Self – Analysis and Stages of Realization

1. Ask group members to think of a time when they felt confused during the quest for an advanced degree, or during educational development.

2. Lead a discussion on Figure 8 & Table 8: "The Student of Color and Stages of Realization."

3. Ask participants to draw a large square, and divide this square into four compartments, similar to Figure 8, like a window pane. Label each pane, according to Figure 8.

4. Direct participants revisit the confusing event initially identified and write a brief description of the event in the "confusion" pane.

5. Ask participants to reflect and note in the appropriate panes, events leading up and following the state of confusion.

6. Have the group share their responses. Discuss: What inferences can be made from this model?

Exercise 3.2: Designing a Personal System of Learning (Note: Can be used separately or in combination with Exercise 3.3.)

1. Have each participant review Figure 10, "Sub-systems with a System of Learning."

2. Have each participant create of diagram, similar to Figure 10, illustrating style, method, or optimum conditions for learning.

3. Conduct a large group discussion, encourage participants to share ideas and make suggestions for improvements.

Exercise 3.3: Nailing Down Positive and Negative Forces that impact Your Learning System

Explain to participants that negative and positive forces co-mingle to create the individual's unique learning situation. Ask participants to look at Figure 11 for an example. Discuss.

> 2.a Ask participants to review diagrams previously created in Exercise 3.2 , reflect, and jot down the positive and negative forces that impact personal learning systems. Or, if using Exercise 3.3 as a stand-alone activity:
>
> 2.b Ask participants to create a single diagram showing the balance between positive and negative forces that impact personal learning systems.
>
> 3. Discuss diagrams in group setting.

Exercise 3.4: Students of Color: How To Create Your Own "Shifting the Burden Story"

> 1. Discuss with participants how it is important to repel stereotypes, beliefs, and assumptions that delay the educational process. Review Figure 14, and Table 10, both labeled "Students of Color: How To Create Your Own "Shifting The Burden Story," with group.
>
> 2. Advise each participant to create their own shifting the burden story. Following steps 1-4 in Table 10.
>
> 3. Have group come together sharing stories, insights, and possible points of leverage for presented stories as shown in Table 10.

Exercise 3.5: Understanding What is Known and Unknown in Problem Diagnosis

> 1. Brainstorm a set of specific problems currently experienced by the group.

2. Direct to group to Figure 15, "The Johari Window," and Table 11, "Student of Color Johari Quadrant Chart." Discuss.

3. Select a brainstormed problem and diagnose as a group. Identify possible ways to bring blind, hidden, or unknown areas in the realm of the known.

4. Allow participants to practice by diagnosing other brainstormed problems. Discuss

<u>You Can and Must Succeed, Here Is Why – *Redefining Success*</u>

Exercise 4.1: Skills Identification Worksheet.

1. Explain to participants that in times of frustration and confusion its important to revisit your foundation to regain clarity and confidence. This exercise allows for a graphic representation of innate and acquired talent and abilities that coalesce to form your foundation.

2. Direct group to Table 18, "<u>Student of Color Achievement Worksheet for Skill Identification.</u> Review worksheet with participants.

3. Advise participants to complete the form. Allow at least 30 minutes.

4. Have participants share and seek feedback on summary read-outs.

Exercise 4.2: Deciding What to Do

1. Explain to participants that this is a holist exercise in that all aspects of the total person is considered when deciding what to do in life. Walk through Table 20, "Deciding What To Do" with participants, providing and eliciting examples where needed.

2. Instruct the participants to draw their own self-analysis chart and provide real-world examples where applicable. If a criterion needs to be addressed, or is not applicable advise participant to mark the field with "N/A."

3. Conduct a group discussion, allowing parties to share their findings, and respond to the findings of others. Encourage the discussion of areas marked "N/A."

Exercise 4.3: Process of Continuous Improvement

1. Discuss Table 22, "Project Sheet: Checklist for Self-Directed Learning" with participants sharing that learning is a continuous process of improvement that starts with the individual.

2. Give participants approximately 10 minutes to complete.

3. Discuss results in large group setting.

Exercise 4.4: Self-Analysis- Steps for Identifying Training and Educational Needs

1. Administer this exercise as a field assignment.

2. Explain that Table 23, "Self-Analysis- Steps for Identifying Training and Educational Needs" takes a behavioral look at skills and talents, then ties this information to training and educational needs. Review with participants.

3. Encourage students to visualize terminal career goals. For participants for who have not decided, encourage exploratory inquiry by suggesting a temporary occupational choice.

4. Have participants conduct field research.

5. Bring participants together again to discuss findings, share insights, and provide suggestions. Can the institution under study provide the skills necessary to reach terminal goals?

Exercise 4.5: Student of Color Strategy For Building a Support Structure

1. Advise participants that it is important to identify and develop a support structure during the acquisition of an advanced degree. Review Table 24, "Student of Color Strategy For Building a Support Structure," with the group.

2. Instruct the group to fill-out the form and discuss results in pairs.

3. Conduct a large group discussion allowing pairs to briefly share their findings.

This section provides the reader with a community-based approach to goal acquisition because the underlying belief is that there is strength in numbers. You are encouraged to create your own group exercises. Many, if not all of these exercises can be adapted for individual use and the reader is encouraged to do so. Being able to have a variety of tools and techniques for overcoming personal and institutional barriers to degree acquisition is imperative. These tools allow us to make order of our circumstances and gain clarity in conditions of chaos. Remember, nothing is beyond your reach.

REFERENCES

Allport, G. W. (1980). The nature of prejudice: the classic study of roots of discrimination. Readings, MA: Addison-Wesley.

Bennet, L. (1962). Before the Mayflower: A history of the Negro in America. Chicago: Johnson.

Bennett, L. (1984). <u>Before the May Flower: A History of Black America, rev.ed</u>. New York: Viking Penguin.

Blauner, R. (1979). <u>Racial oppression in america.</u> New York: Harper & Row.

Bollman, L. G., & Deal T. E. (1984). <u>Modern approaches to understanding and managing organizations.</u> San Francisco: Jossey-Bass.

Capra, F. (1996). <u>Web of life</u>. New York: Anchor Books.

Comer, J. P. (1972). <u>Beyond Black and White</u>. New York: Quadrangle Books.

Comer, J. (1988). Educating poor minority children. <u>Scientific American, 259,</u> 42-48.

Czarny, F. S. (2001). <u>African-American families of incarcerated males: an emergent study of orchestrated leadership.</u> Doctoral dissertation, Fielding Institute, California.

Davie, M. R. (1949). <u>Negroes in American society.</u> New York: McGraw-Hill.

Ducas, G. & Van Doren, C. (1970). <u>Great documents in Black American history.</u> American history. New York: Praeger.

Dye, T. R. (1998). <u>Understanding public policy</u>. Saddle River, NJ: Prentice Hall.

Elkins, S. M. (1963). <u>Slavery: A problem in American institutional</u> and intellectual life. 2nd ed. Chicago: University of Chicago Press.

Gatti, R. D. & Gatti, D. J. (1983). <u>The new encyclopedic dictionary of school law</u>. West Nyack, New York: Parker.

Goldfield, D. R. (1990). <u>Black, White, and southern</u>. Baton Rouge, LA: Louisiana State University Press.

Horton, J. O. & Horton, L. E. (1995). A history of the African American people. New York, NY: SMITHMARK Publishers.

Huges, L. (1962). Fight for freedom: The story of the NAACP. New York: Norton.

Jennings, P. & Brewster, T. (1998). The century. New York, NY: Doubleday.

Kelly A. H. & Harbison, W.A. (1970). The American constitution: Its origins & development. New York, NY: W. W. Norton & Company, Inc.

McClenney, E.H. (1987). <u>How to survive when you're the only black in the office.</u> First Associates Publishing: Richmond Virginia.

McLemore, S. D. (1991). Racial and ethnic relations in America. Boston, MA: Allyn and Bacon.

Mink, O. C., Esterhuysen, P. W., Mink, B. P., & Owen, K. Q. (1993). <u>Change at work: a comprehensive management process for transforming organizations.</u> San Francisco: Jossey-Bass.

Mydral, G. (1944). An American delima: The Negro problem and modern democracy. New York: Harper.

Natemeyer, H., & Gilberg, J. (1989). <u>Classics of organizational behavior.</u> (2nd ed.). Danville: Interstate.

Ploski, H. A. & Brown, R. C. (1967). The Negro almanac. New York: Bellswether.

Proctor, S. D. (1980). "Equality from a racial/ethnic perspective." The NationalCenter for

    Research in Vocational Education. Columbus, Ohio: National Center Publications,

    Box F.

Saenger, G. (1953). The social psychology of prejudice. New York: Harper.

Senge. P.M. (1990). The fifth discipline. New York: Doubleday.

Smith, R.M. (1982). Learning how to learn. New York: Free Press.

Stevens-Long, J., & Commons, M. L. (1992). Adult life. Mountainview, California:

    Mayfield Publishing Company.

Weisbord, M. (1992). Discovering common ground. San Francisco: Berrett-Koehler.

Wilkinson, B. (1997). The civil rights movement: An illustrated history. New York, NY:

    Random House.

Woodson, C. G. (1935). The story of the Negro retold. Washington, D.C.: The Associated

    Press.

About the Authors

Dr. Frank S. Czarny, a black African American, earned a Ph.D. in Human and Organizational Systems. Included in Who's Who in America, Dr. Czarny helps individuals and groups resolve conflict in a variety of educational and industrial settings. Using a systems-based approach, Dr. Czarny assists clients create and implement action plans related to multicultural communication, racism, ageism, and gender issues.

C.J.H. Dorsey completed her Ed.D. in Educational Leadership and Change. She is a black African American with 28 ½ years of state level experience working for the State of Washington, Office of Superintendent of Public Instruction, Olympia WA. Dr. Dorsey has developed and implemented statewide educational training programs, human relation workshops, and civil rights and discrimination conferences in educational environments.